The Fourpenny Axe and a Snooker Cue

Garth Alperstein

The Fourpenny Axe and a Snooker Cue
eBofolo Remembered

The Fourpenny Axe and a Snooker Cue: eBofolo Remembered
ISBN 978 1 76041 034 6
Copyright © text Garth Alperstein 2015
Cover design: Victor Gordon, John Stahel, Melissa Becker, Sauce Design

First published 2015 by
GINNINDERRA PRESS
PO Box 3461 Port Adelaide 5015
www.ginninderrapress.com.au

Dedicated to

Melissa, Dion, Lucien and all the inhabitants
of Fort Beaufort past and present, real and fictitious

Union of South Africa, 1910–1961.

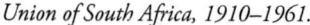

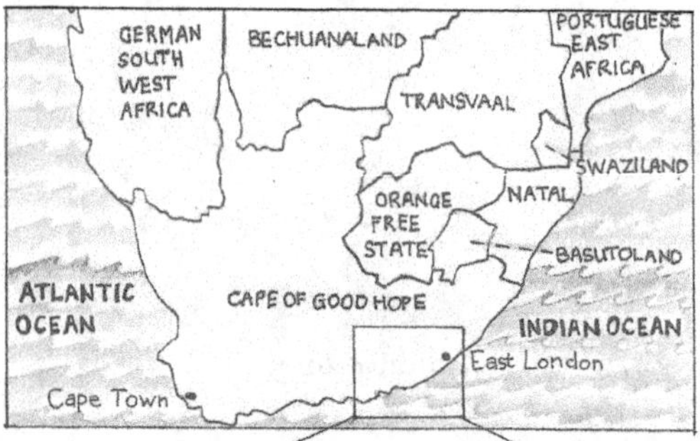

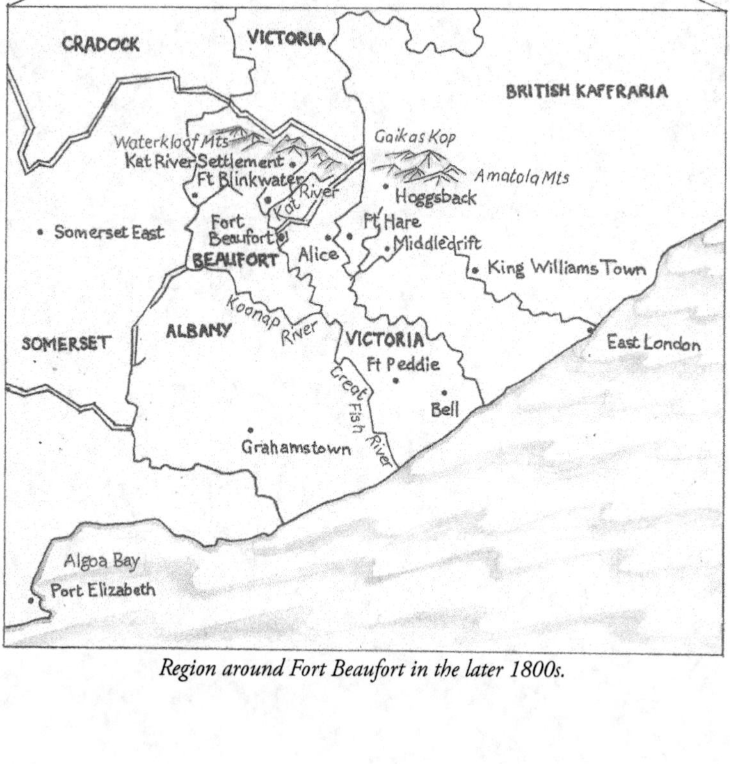

Region around Fort Beaufort in the later 1800s.

Preface

I was born in 1950 in a small town in the Eastern Cape, South Africa, to a Jewish family who had fled the pogroms in Russia and Eastern Europe at the end of the nineteenth century. The town was started as a military outpost by the British colonial government in the 1822 and was named Fort Beaufort. The Xhosa people of the area called it eBofolo.

I started writing my story as a memoir. I wrote about the strange, comic and sometimes violent life of a small town with much racism during the harsh apartheid years and the effects over two generations on my displaced family.

The main storyline is my description of characters and events, from comic to tragic, in Fort Beaufort, as I recall them. Most of the story is set between 1953 and 1968 – from when I was three through my teenage years. During most of this period, my father was the mayor. I describe how my perceptions evolved and changed as I grew up. Where appropriate, the names of some people have been changed to protect their identity.

Gradually I became interested in the history of Fort Beaufort itself. Why was it there and what had been there before it? I researched its history, most of which was new to me, as we had been given a very limited and biased version in school. I then wove into my memoir fictionalised stories of the San (Bushmen), the Khoikhoi (Hottentots) and the Xhosa, who all inhabited the region before the arrival of the British and the Afrikaners. Their arrival resulted in many violent clashes with the indigenous people. These fictionalised stories are not accurate historical accounts, but attempts to provide some context for and flavour of the historical background. They are intended to provide small windows into the past, and link to my experience as a child growing up in Fort Beaufort.

I am conscious that the stories of the San, Khoikhoi, Xhosa and early Europeans are based on historical and anthropological writings which probably have a strong European bias and may contain inaccurate representations of these peoples.

When I was growing up during the apartheid era in South Africa, all people were officially classified by the government according to its perception of 'race'. These categories were partly based on a complex system of visual appearance – facial features, hair and skin colour. The categories were 'black', 'coloured' and 'white'. If one did not appear European or black African, one was classified as 'coloured'. This group included the Khoikhoi and the San, Cape Malays from Indonesia, Indians from India, Chinese and mixed-race people. However, there were anomalies. Japanese people were classified as 'honorary whites' possibly because of trade links. Many people of Middle Eastern ancestry were classified as 'white' despite many having darker skin colour than those classified as 'coloured'.

Many families were split up because of the difference in appearance amongst them, and their children attended different schools. It was also illegal for the various groups to cohabit or have sexual relationships. Although this classification system is no longer in use, I have used the terms 'black', 'white' and 'coloured' in inverted commas because they were in use during the period in which my story was set.

1

Of burnt-out buildings
Many stories to tell
Lost in smoke

It is 1996. I look at the remnants of Deane's Commercial Hotel in Fort Beaufort, South Africa. The brick and cement shell of the building is still intact and the upstairs balcony still visible, but the roof is gone. The building has obvious fire damage with soot on the walls. Doors and windows are boarded up. The liquor store, called the Off Sales, attached to the hotel, is now a small clothes shop. Xhosa and 'coloured' women and men crowd the streets and footpaths, some selling goods on colourful mats. Unlike the Fort Beaufort of my childhood, I see few 'white' people.

Across the street, the town hall clock is stuck on twenty to two. Next to the town hall, the park is overgrown with grass and bushes. Litter clings to the maze of elephant grass hedges. My brother Neil, my sister Melanie and I stand in front of our burnt-down memory. It is a sultry, overcast day.

'Excuse me, would you please take a photograph of us in front of this building?' requests Neil of a young Xhosa woman.

Hesitantly, she takes my brother's camera from his hand, looking perplexed. Through the lens she focuses her gaze on the three people, two men and a woman, standing in front of the ruin of the hotel. In an awkward silence, the wind rustles plastic bags littering the street. A few yards away, a stray dog nonchalantly chews on chicken bones in the gutter. The woman steadies the camera and presses the button.

*

On a summer's day in 1816, Reverend Joseph Williams of the London Missionary Society stands outside his newly established mission station near the Kat River. He can hear in the distance the Hadeda ibis making its characteristic har-dee-dar call. His main purpose is to convert Chief Maqoma and his tribe to Christianity. But this is not the beginning of Fort Beaufort.

In the distance he sees a number of people approaching on horseback. He recognises the person leading the group. It is his dear friend Lord Charles Somerset, Governor of the Cape Province. The group arrives and dismounts.

'Lord Somerset, to what do I owe this honour?'

'Good day to you, Reverend.'

'Do come in for a cup of tea, sir, and please invite your men as well.'

The two men enter the building, followed closely by Somerset's entourage. They sit at a large wooden table covered with a tartan tablecloth. The room is small and dark, with light entering two windows on the north side.

A few minutes later, a young African woman enters with a china teapot and teacups on a silver tray, and places it on the table. She is wearing a black cloth headdress, beaded necklaces, beaded bracelets and anklets, but is otherwise scantily clothed. Lord Somerset's men, being conscious of the reverend in the room, try not to look at her directly.

'Enkosi – thank you, Nomondi,' says Reverend Williams.

She pours the tea and leaves the room.

'Reverend, as you are aware, I have met with Chief Maqoma on a number of occasions to negotiate the cessation of cattle theft from the white farmers,' says Lord Somerset. He frowns. 'He clearly has no intention of complying with my requests. I am now forced to take action. I will order Colonel Maurice Scott to establish a military post three miles from here on the other side of the Kat River.'

'Yes, of course, sir. I look forward to a cordial relationship with Colonel Scott.'

Lord Somerset leaves with his men following, all turning their heads to peer through the kitchen window as they return to their horses.

*

Six years later, Colonel Maurice Scott of the Royal Warwickshire Regiment stands proudly in front of a rectangular stone building on top of the hill. After a long hot summer, the earth is parched. A warm wind stirs up swirls of dust that move swiftly across the ground then fade away as fast as they appear. Colonel Scott is dressed in his full military regalia. Before him is a small platoon of soldiers, wearing red-and-black uniforms. He twirls both sides of his moustache and clears his throat. As if on cue, the soldiers become silent.

'Men,' he announces, 'the blockhouse is now complete. We will have a strong fortress here against the raids by the Xhosa chief, Jongumsobomvu Maqoma. We are now strategically placed, as we are almost surrounded by the Kat and Brak Rivers in a horseshoe shape.' Scott stops and stares at his men with unusual intensity before adding, 'Except to the north.' Pointing now with his cane at the map set up on the makeshift table before him, he raps the cane on the area of the map where the rivers run and announces, 'Soon we will be in total control of the region when we build a couple of bridges across them.' He pauses. He looks up towards the sky, as if he is going to address the heavens. 'And now, in the name of Lord Charles Somerset, and in honour of his father, the Duke of Beaufort, I name this settlement Fort Beaufort.'

His platoon of soldiers, staring straight ahead, present arms.

In the distance, in the shadow of a mimosa thorn tree, only the whites of the eyes of a black man can be seen.

2

> At the beginning
> The song sometimes
> Hears the end

The hill on the south side of town, called Kiss Me Quick, provides a good bird's-eye view of Fort Beaufort. When I was young, it was a favourite place for young couples to park after dark in their parents' old Buick or Ford Zephyr and snog in the back seat.

Three bridges span the Kat and Brak rivers, which snake around the town in a horseshoe shape, with the open part of the horseshoe to the north.

Fort Beaufort is built on a neat grid with a town square in the middle. Other than in the bars of the three hotels (Deane's, the Savoy and the Royal), in my day, the hub of most activity occurred around the town square. It was surrounded by shops, banks and the town hall, which also housed the council chambers and the Kit Kat Cinema.

In the middle of town, opposite the town hall, on top of the hill upon which Fort Beaufort was built, stood Deane's Hotel, my parents' hotel, and my home.

*

I was born to Max and Rose Alperstein on a Thursday at about eight o'clock in the morning on 13 April 1950 in Fort Beaufort, Cape Province, Union of South Africa, a citizen of planet Earth, Milky Way galaxy, but I am not sure of which multiverse I am a member. I say about eight o'clock because in Fort Beaufort, time had a different meaning. The time would have been rounded off to the nearest fifteen minutes or maybe even half an hour.

I do not remember being born, but in my more fanciful moments I think I can recall the feeling of being born. It was quite cosy till I was held upside down by the ankles and smacked on the bottom, as was then the custom. My mother said that when I was born she felt as if she was the only woman in the world who had ever given birth. My next memory was crying. Or maybe it was purely imagined after my mother told me I cried a lot in my first few months of life, especially at night. She said she sat up for hours with me at night, smoking one cigarette after the other. Probably choking on the smoke, I thought. No wonder I cried so much. Maybe I just cried because babies cry.

In another fanciful moment, after my mother had told me that I was a real 'pain in the neck' to take to the beach when I was a toddler, I thought I maybe, possibly, perhaps could remember that I did not like walking on the sea sand. She said she had to carry me across the beach and then put me on a towel from which I would not move.

However, my first clear memory is from when I was three.

*

I stand, rubbing my eyes, in the corner of the kitchen of Deane's Hotel in eBofolo. It's early evening. The sun is going down. My third birthday party is over. About forty of my friends and I have eaten sweets and cake, drunk Hubbly Bubbly, played 'pin the donkey' and made a lot of noise running around the hotel.

The smell of roast beef is yummy. There's a big kitchen that has two levels. At the bottom is a coal oven and stove that is as big as the whole back wall. The walls are painted the same green colour I saw in the hospital where my sister, Melanie, was born. Ivy Nqobo, the chief cook, walks slowly up the sloping concrete ramp to the upper level, to the pantry. Ivy is short and fat, and has a round face and smiles all the time. The fridge in the pantry is big enough for our whole family to sleep in.

Ivy pulls out a whole cow's leg from the fridge and walks back to the table in front of the stove, carrying the leg on her shoulder. As she cuts into the meat, she starts singing *Nkosi, sikelel' iAfrika* very loudly. Edward Makabane and all the kitchen workers join in harmony together, while they are busy making the dinner. They sing *Nkosi, sikelel' iAfrika, Malupakam'upondo lwayo*, all the way to the end of the song. I feel funny. I do not know what this feeling is about.

'Come, Garth, I think you've had enough for one day. It's time for you to have a bath and go to bed,' says my mom, leading me by the hand.

*

As I now recall that event as an adult, them singing the African national anthem felt like power, like cohesion, inner strength, survival, like knowing that some day their time would come.

*

One morning, around 6000 BCE, the ground is still cold. A young San boy lies curled up, his back against his mother's warm stomach as she sleeps. A red circle emerges above the parched hill. Dark outlines of mimosa thorn trees and other grey-green shrubs slowly begin to emerge. A river in the shape of a horseshoe surrounds them, except to the north. The air is still. For a moment there is silence. Then a raucous twitter of birds begins. He is hungry. He feels the stomach pains again. Slender rays of sun begin to stream through the leaves and branches of the scanty sleeping shelter that form a loose dome over them. His mother puts her arm around him. His father has been away, hunting. The sun has come up four times since he's left.

'/ûre. Kaise a !gau //goaga xuige – Stop squirming. It's still too early to get up.' His mother tightens the little deerskin leather belt around his abdomen. She knows he is hungry. She tightens her own belt.

Quite suddenly, the sun bursts over the hill and aloe spears shine bright red, contained only by the thick green fleshy leaves edged by rows of sharp thorns. *A young kudu deer with its long curved and twisted horns startles and rapidly disappears.*

He lies there a little while longer, then gently slides out of his mother's arm and along the ground like a cobra and through the entrance of the shelter.

*

It is the morning after my third birthday. I wake up early and lie in bed, waiting for my nanny, Beauty Baardman, to arrive. Beauty is short and walks with her bum sticking out. She is wearing a blue uniform and a white shirt that looks very bright on her black skin. She has a small white doek on her head covering her very short curled black hair.

'*Molo kwedini. Kunjani* – Hello, young boy. How are you?'

'*Ndiphilile* – I'm well, Beauty. Can we go to the train station, *namhlanje* – today?'

'Yes, but you must first get dressed.'

I love going to the train station to watch trains and the people who work on them. I watch the man with the small metal hammer tap all the wheels, listening carefully with his ear close to the wheel, and the man who pulls the levers to make the rails switch tracks.

Near the railway station and the Fort Beaufort Hospital is a fort, the Martello tower. It is round, two storeys high and has a big cannon on top.

To get to the station, we walk past my friend Malcolm Keevy's house. His dad is our doctor. We go past the Martello tower next to the house of the superintendent of the mental hospital. He has two children. They each sit in wheelchairs and dribble all day and can't talk, only make noises. My mom says the superintendent and his wife are cousins. We pass the co-op packing shed where we sometimes buy big pockets of oranges for twenty pennies.

Finally, we come to the station.

'Beauty, when is the train coming?'

'Well, there is only one train today. It is Tuesday, and it comes at about eleven o'clock.'

'Is that a long time from now?'
'It is ten to eight now.'
'OK, let's wait.'

3

Keyboard and pen
The story begins
Slow step

Melissa and I are hiking in a forest about an hour north of New York City, in the summer of 1981, four years after having left our birthplace, South Africa. I evaded a compulsory military call-up. It is a very hot and humid day. We scramble up a slope next to a rapidly running brook surrounded on both sides by dense, subtropical undergrowth. I'm telling her stories again from my childhood growing up in Fort Beaufort. Since we met in 1970, I have been telling her these stories.

'You have to write these down,' she says, being a city person from Port Elizabeth and fascinated by village life. But they remain as anecdotes until the second half of the 90s, some fifteen years later. By this time, we have two children, and are living in Sydney, Australia. These anecdotes also become bedtime stories to our children, Dion and Lucien. A number of events occur before I finally put pen to paper or, more precisely, fingers to keyboard.

During the latter part of the 80s and early 90s, as the apartheid era comes to an end, Fort Beaufort progressively becomes a more overtly 'black' town. In March 1994, my parents' hotel, the one in the photo taken by the Xhosa woman, burns down. Within two months, in South Africa's first democratically held elections, Nelson Mandela is elected the first 'black' president of the Republic of South Africa. The symbolism of these events becomes too much for me to ignore. For the first time, I become interested in the history of Fort Beaufort.

The literature on South Africa is vast, with conflicting perspectives, but I find very little information specifically on Fort Beaufort itself. In addition to my memories of characters and events in that town, I elect to use my imagination in describing historical events loosely based on what I have read.

Working full time, I only occasionally have time to write. I do most of my writing for very short periods during school holidays, some of which we spend in Hawk's Nest, a small seaside town about four hours' drive north of Sydney. The living room of the house we stay in faces Port Stephens Bay, calm as a lake and surrounded by fine yellow sea sand. The entrance to the bay is punctuated by a rocky headland on both the north and south sides, each covered with gum trees and coastal shrub. Beyond the bay is the crystal-clear turquoise water of the Pacific Ocean. It is far away from Fort Beaufort and my memories, but the setting is conducive to writing.

4

> Purple blue bells
> Beneath the trees lie
> Still hidden the heat of summer

I wake up early on a summer's day in 1954. I can smell the jasmine flowers. I look outside and watch the sun rise. It is red like the colour of the bricks at the brick factory where I sometimes play. There are jacaranda trees everywhere in the streets and their purple flowers fall on the ground. In contrast, the mountains around Fort Beaufort have only a few mimosa thorn trees, aloes and small green and grey bushes on them.

Melanie is still asleep in the other bed in our small bedroom that is next to my parents' room. Our room leads into an even smaller one where we keep our clothes and toys. The noisy fan is still blowing warm air around the room.

Through the closed door I hear my dad, Max, say to my mom, 'I don't think I'll bother to shave today, Rose. It's too hot.'

There is no reply from my mom.

I jump out of bed and open the door. 'Daddy, can we go and have breakfast?'

'After I've showered. I'm all sweaty from the heat last night. The fan didn't help much. I think we'll sleep out on the balcony tonight if it's this hot again.'

On the second storey of the hotel our family has three bedrooms, a small enclosed balcony leading off my parents' bedroom, and a large flat open balcony area which is the roof above the bars and liquor shop. My father built a brick *braaivleis* – barbecue – on the rooftop where we *braai* chops, steak and *boerewors* – sausage. On hot nights we carry our mattresses onto the roof, and, smeared with citronella oil to keep the mozzies away, we sleep under the stars.

'I'll come and shower. I'm sweaty too.'

We walk down the long corridor past all the guest rooms.

When we reach the toilet, my dad says, 'I just have to pay a visit to parliament.' He always says that when he goes to the toilet.

I wait outside. I hear him light a cigarette. Five minutes later, he opens the toilet door and a disgusting combination of smells hits me. We finally get to the shower room, which is big enough to live in, and which has a showerhead large enough for three people to get wet at the same time. The shower room has a very big light bulb. It is double the size of a regular light bulb and has a large zigzag filament. I like to stare at the bright light.

*

I do most of my writing in cafés near where we live in Sydney. I find I can concentrate better with some ambient noise; when I was at university I used to study with the radio playing.

We live ten minutes' walk from Coogee Beach, where there are a number of cafés with views of Coogee Bay. I often get inspired when staring at the calm blue sea with the waves gently breaking on the pale sand.

I am pondering the life of the San in the Fort Beaufort region and have read a number of books on their history, lifestyle, myths and legends. There is a story about the moonlight blinding a praying mantis, which, tangentially, reminds me of that bright light bulb in the shower that never died. The bulb is present when my parents buy the hotel in 1948 and is still functioning when the hotel is sold twenty-five years later. The story of its longevity passes into family legend.

*

On the same hill, almost surrounded by river, around 4000 BCE, a young

San child is squatting on the ground next to his grandmother. He has a twig in his hand and is flicking a small praying mantis with it. The sun is setting. It is near the horizon and looks like a bright orange ball. The air is still. His mother is cooking a piece of kudu deer meat on a stick over a small fire. The smell is making him hungry.

'Tats ge ni !aedaga ≠û – You must never eat the mantis,' says his grandmother. There is a long pause. 'Gaxu //aeb !kharuhase – A long time ago...' She pauses again.

The boy looks up at her. He knows his grandmother is going to tell a story.

She starts again, '...the mantis wanted to jump onto the moon so that all the other animals and insects would think that he was a god, and that they should all praise him. He climbed up a rock and he climbed up trees, trying to jump onto the moon, but it kept rising up into the sky without him. One day he saw the moon in the water. He was so angry that he couldn't jump onto the moon, that he threw a rock at it.'

The young boy flicks the mantis into the air and catches it again very deftly with the stick. The mantis clings to it.

'/ûre – Stop that! I'm telling you a story. Listen. When the mantis threw the rock into the water, a thousand splinters of moonlight pierced its eyes. He couldn't sleep because there was no darkness in his eyes. He no longer wanted to be a god sitting on the moon. So he put his two front legs up before him, stood on his back legs and prayed to the moon to give him back his eyesight. After praying for many days, he woke up one morning and could see the birds clearly again. The moon had given him back his eyesight. That is why today the mantis still holds up his front legs to praise the moon for giving him back his eyesight.'

The young boy looks up at his grandmother and smiles.

'Enough stories now. Come, it is time to eat,' says his grandmother.

*

After showering we go back to the bedroom, and my dad puts on a short-sleeved khaki shirt, khaki short pants and brown sandals. He wears the same clothes and sandals every day in summer.

Beauty walks into the bedroom.

'*Molo*, Beauty,' I greet her.

She looks around at the mess in the room and scowls at my dad. '*Mlungu* – Master – how many times must I tell you not to put your dirty clothes on the floor next to the wardrobe. You know they should be next to the chair.'

He doesn't say anything.

My mom and Melanie are up and dressed. We all walk to the dining room for breakfast, down the staircase, past the 'ladies lounge' that has not yet been cleaned and that stinks of gin and stale cigarette smoke. On the tables in the lounge are ashtrays filled with cigarette butts, ash and empty glasses, some half-filled with flat beer. One of the chairs has a fresh stain where Baas Bob, who comes to the hotel to drink everyday, has wet his pants after falling asleep. He often does that. I sniff the chair. I can still smell wee, even after my mom has said to the lounge cleaner that she must 'make sure you get the piss smell out'.

We are first in the dining room except for the Rowley sisters. The Rowley sisters have lived in the hotel for many years. They always sit in the corner of the dining room facing the courtyard. My mom says that neither of them ever married. They both smoke cigarettes all day and speak with deep rough voices like many of the old men who come to the pub. This year, old Miss Rowley will be ninety, and young Miss Rowley will be eighty-eight.

We order our usual breakfast: two or three fried eggs, crisp bacon, fried tomato and a sausage, white toast smeared thick with butter and Boereplaas coffee. Sometimes we also have fried sheep's kidneys and steak, and sometimes calf's liver and onions as well. In winter we often start with Jungle Oats porridge covered with spoonfuls of white sugar, a large blob of butter and milk.

Every morning my mom starts breakfast with the crossword from the *Daily Dispatch*, which she calls the Daily Disgrace, and a cigarette in a thin black holder. She always finishes the puzzle before the end of breakfast. She says the crossword is too difficult for me still, because it is a cryptic crossword, whatever that is.

Her cigarette smoke starts drifting my way. I grab the largest cereal box and put it between the smoke and me.

'You bloody kids make me sick.'

'Your smoke makes me cough and it stinks.'

'Jesus wept, I can't even have breakfast in peace!'

I take the Worcestershire sauce bottle and shake a few drops onto my fried eggs.

*

When as a medical student, I learn about the harmful effects of cigarette smoking, and am giving my mother a lecture on smoking, she cuts me short.

'If there is one good thing I have done in my life, it is put you off smoking, so SHUT UP!'

I am silenced.

*

After breakfast, my dad opens up the pub, as he does every day, and starts to get ready for the first customers at ten o'clock. Every morning when he opens the doors, that same smell of old cigarette smoke and a mixture of beer, whisky, brandy and cane spirits comes out into the courtyard.

5

> Twists and turns of fate
> Spiral in and out
> Of the ribbon of life

I now wish that I had found out a lot more about my parents' lives. However, I am conscious that my own children, as young adults, have other things to occupy their minds, and that the details of our histories are currently not a priority. Maybe it is more the norm for that interest to occur later in life.

My father was born on a farm near Middledrift in 1915 to Gutel and Keila Alperstein. Middledrift is even smaller than Fort Beaufort, about half an hour's drive away on a very bumpy dirt road.

My grandmother, who we called Granny Tzatzke, liked to say that, when my father was born, he came out quickly, 'like a football'. She said that she was sure he was going to be a good rugby player. She was right.

He went to boarding school at Dale College in King Williams Town, fifty miles from Fort Beaufort. At school he played rugby, cricket and tennis for the school's first teams. When he went to Rhodes University in Grahamstown (also about fifty miles from Fort Beaufort), he not only played first team rugby and cricket, but was also chairman of the bridge club and became the university bridge champion. Hence, he took five years to complete a three-year Bachelor of Arts degree.

Then came the Second World War, and my father enlisted. He fought in the heavy artillery section with the Allies in north Africa and southern Europe. My father spoke little of the war to us children, but one story he did tell that sticks in my mind was about a flight he took from Italy to

Egypt on his way back to South Africa when the war ended. He boarded the airplane, and when it was about to take off, an announcement was made that one particular soldier was desperate to make this earlier flight; would anyone volunteer to take a later flight? My father volunteered. The next day he learned that the plane had crashed into the Mediterranean Sea. There were no survivors. When I was young, I asked if we would still have been born if he had been killed. He said no.

After the war, he got a job teaching Latin and English at Selbourne College (the boarding school where I was later sent) in East London, South Africa's fifth biggest city, halfway up the east coast, about eighty-five miles from Fort Beaufort. While in East London, he and my mother, Rose Cooper, married. She was teaching bookkeeping and accounting at the technical college. They earned very little money teaching, and both wanted to do something else. An opportunity came from my mother's father, Philip Cooper, who suggested he sell his little inn at Bell and together they buy a hotel. At the time, they had a choice of the Highgate Hotel on the outskirts of East London or Deane's Commercial Hotel in Fort Beaufort. According to my mother, my father was a bit of a romantic, a touch impulsive, and liked the idea of a country hotel, so in 1948, two years before I was born, they bought Deane's.

In that year, the Nationalist Party, which formalised apartheid, came into power.

*

It is just after lunch. My dad is having a rest on his bed. I am lying next to him. I have a Noddy book in my hand. I love Noddy books. I get totally lost in the world of Big Ears, Noddy, Mr Plod and all the other characters. I imagine all the buildings in town looking like those in the books – colourful wooden blocks – and all the cars look like Noddy's car, a little red and yellow bubble car.

'Dad, will you read me a Noddy book?'

'Yes, Toto, if you pass me my cigarettes on the bedside table next to you.'

Toto is one of my nicknames. My dad told *Oom* – Uncle – Hendrik that when I was learning to speak I used to say 'toto' all the time.

I look at the cigarette box next to me. I get up off the bed, walk over to the electric bell on the doorframe between his bedroom and ours and press it. All the rooms in the hotel have bells so that guests can call a waiter to their room. My mom says it is room service. I get back onto the bed to hear the Noddy story. My dad looks at me with a funny look on his face. There is a knock at the door.

'*Ngena* – Come in,' I shout.

Edward the waiter walks in. '*Ewe, Mlungu* – Yes, Master,' he says, looking at my dad.

'Edward, can you pass the Master his cigarettes,' I say, just like dad, pointing to the box on the bedside table next to me.

Edward walks over to my side of the bed, picks up the cigarettes, walks around the bed and gives them to my dad.

My dad has a look on his face I don't understand, and then bursts out laughing. I don't know what he is laughing at. He always orders the waiters around and everyone else in the hotel. I see him doing that all the time.

*

To this day, I am both appalled and embarrassed by that event. As an adult, I have been able to work out how my behaviour and attitude at age four might have evolved.

The more I read about how the history of South Africa and the Fort Beaufort region was censored at school, the more I am able to understand how such a divided society and the apartheid system developed. Although the Nationalist government has been held most responsible for apartheid (separate development), between 1884 and 1946 the British colonial government passed seventeen Bills and Acts relating to separate development. These included the Hut Tax in 1884, which forced 'black' people into work; the Native Land Act in 1913, allotting 13% of the land to 'black' people and 87% to 'white' people; and the Immorality Act in 1927, forbidding sexual relations between 'black' and 'white' people.

I am intrigued by some of the writings, which attempt to portray a Xhosa perspective on aspects of the early history, particularly in relation to the arrival of the British.

*

Chief Jongumsobomvu Maqoma, renowned Ngqika Chief of the amaRarabe Kingdom, is sitting in his kraal in the summer of 1824, in the shade of a tree near the Kat River, surrounded by a number of tribal elders. He has a leopard skin on his back, with the front legs hanging over his shoulders. He holds a spear in his right hand. The atmosphere is tense.

He looks at his witchdoctor. 'What do you know about all the "white" men arriving in eBaai – Algoa Bay?'

'Many people, men and women, have come from far away by boat. They wear heavy clothes, even when it is hot.'

This comment results in much amusement. '

I have also been told they have powerful guns that can kill a man with one shot.'

'Auk! Hayi – No!' *exclaims one of the elders.*

'Have they come to stay, or have they just come to trade with us?'

'With so many women, they must have come to stay, I think, Chief Maqoma.'

'Why did the white man come here?'

'It is said that the white man killed their God, nailed him on a tree, and so had to look for new lands.'

He shakes his head from side to side, grinning in disbelief.

'Hayi! Uthixo! – No, God!' *exclaims the same elder. He chews on a piece of dried meat in his right hand, swallows, clears his throat, then spits on the ground.*

The others join in, shaking their heads.

6

> Many contradictions
> Hide behind
> Fine words and rhyme

Much about my father I only learned in my latter adult years while doing some research into our family history and ancestry. He was an imposing man: six foot tall and weighing two hundred and forty pounds. He always had a very short haircut with no-back-and-sides and a middle parting. He had a large double chin, and a bulging abdomen to match. From what I recall, my father mostly had a worried, sad expression on his face, but was still capable of many a loud belly laugh.

Max served as a municipal councillor for a few years before becoming mayor of Fort Beaufort in 1955. His induction as mayor took the form of a public Jewish religious service at Fort Beaufort, conducted by the Rev. Y. Kemelman of East London, South Africa, in English, Afrikaans and Hebrew. Max served as mayor for ten years.

He was a Jewish agnostic in the English camp of a predominantly Afrikaner town, and an open supporter of the United Party, the main opposition to the governing Nationalist Party, which was predominantly supported by Afrikaners. Maybe they voted for him because he also drank like the boys, was active in the rugby club, and called 'black' people 'savages' and 'Kaffirs'. Maybe it was because he got things done for the town. Max did modernise the sewage system. Before that, there were certain nights when people would have to put their toilet buckets in the street and the 'honey cart', as we called it, drove around the town and emptied them. Bigger buildings like the hotels had large underground sewage pits, which were emptied by pumping the sewage through a large pipe into the honey cart. The driver of the vehicle was invariably 'white', but the people who emptied the buckets and handled the pump hose were always 'black'. We kids often followed the honey cart around town, both repulsed and at the same time curiously fascinated by the smell.

I recall one year when Clarrie Bezuidenhout, the town clerk and a staunch Nationalist supporter, stood against my father. Max still won by a large majority. My father had a soft spot for Clarrie's wife, Sanna. He said she made the best *melktert* – custard tart – in Fort Beaufort.

Having studied to be an English and Latin teacher, my father would often quote Shakespeare, Catullus and many others, at the most unexpected moments. After one of my sister's tantrums, during her peak tantrum phase, at about three years of age, I recall him raising his hands above and placing them at the back of his head, looking towards the sky and then with an anguished look on his face, saying, 'How sharper than a serpent's tooth it is to have a thankless child,' quoting from King Lear.

When I started studying poetry in high school, my father would take the opportunity to quote lines from the many poems he knew by heart. Holding a glass of champagne in his hand he would start, 'Oh, for a beaker of the warm South! Full of the true, the blushful Hippocrene, with beaded bubbles winking at the brim,' and continue to quote the whole of the 'Ode to a Nightingale', by Keats.

Max was also into drama and having fun. During his years as mayor, he organised a number of carnival days. All the 'whites' in the town took part and spent months building elaborate floats that were driven through the streets on trucks and tractors. The 'black' and 'coloured' people were allowed to be spectators only. One year he sat on the town council float dressed in a large floral dress. For breasts he had two massive balloons. He wore a lady's wide-brimmed hat and his usual brown leather sandals.

*

After lunch, I tease Melanie and dare her to try to catch me. I know where to hide – the front lounge. She will never guess I am hiding there. I run to the front of the hotel. The lounge door is shut. I open the door, and quickly shut it behind me. I see my dad is sitting on a chair with a glass of whisky in his hand, and across from him is a young Xhosa man, wearing a blue blazer, a white shirt and a tie. He has a beer in his hand.

'Garthie, this is Mr Makapuma. He's a teacher at the Healdtown school. We are busy. Go and play.'

'But Dad, I'm hiding from Melanie.'

'Go and hide somewhere else then.'

My dad says 'black' people are savages. Why is he drinking with a black man in the lounge? Roger Crane said he would never drink sitting next to a Kaffir in the bar. He also said 'black' people aren't allowed to drink in the hotel. My dad will get into trouble with the police.

*

I have not been able to find out precisely when Deane's was built. I had thought that my father had once told me that Deane's Hotel was originally an army barracks, which then got converted into a brewery, then an inn and finally a hotel.

*

Private Buck Adams is sitting at a rickety wooden table in the tavern diagonally opposite the town square. He is on his third ale. Flies buzz around his face. It is February 1844 and they have had no rain for six months now. Despite the heat, he enjoys his warm ale. Reverend Calderwood walks into the bar, and takes off his hat. His sweaty hair is plastered down onto his head and sweat drips down his neck and face.

'Do join me for an ale, Reverend,' invites Adams. 'How is the missionary work among Maqoma and his tribe going?'

Reverend Calderwood sits down opposite Adams. The barman brings him a warm ale in a large glass and places it carefully on the table.

'Very well, thank you, Private Adams. I have the utmost respect for Chief Maqoma, but he is still somewhat resistant to converting to Christianity, and until he does, his tribe won't. However, he is a man of principles, a dignified man who has a strong belief in his own God and ancestors. When he finds our God, I believe he will be a good Christian.'

'Reverend Calderwood, did you hear that this past Sunday Maqoma came to town with his wives and at least twenty of his men, as he has done on many an occasion, and drank all day and all night until the sun came up. Maqoma was the first to get drunk. They were all unashamedly naked. One of his wives got so drunk they took her to the river and kept dipping her in till she sobered up. Frightful sight it was. He has been quite the drunkard for the past ten years.'

'Well, yes, I have heard these stories about Maqoma being a drunkard, but I have never seen him partake on his land with his people,' replies the reverend emphatically.

*

A year later, Chief Maqoma is sitting on his haunches on a large rock in the Waterkloof Mountains. As a mark of his status, a leopard skin covers his shoulders. Behind him sit his twenty-seven wives, and in front, the two hundred men he has taken with him, after the British had forced him off his land in the Amatola Mountains and the Kat River valley for the third time.

'We will be safe here deep in the forest. The British soldiers will find it difficult to find us through the thorn trees, monkey ropes and the many caves. We will no longer fight the British in the open veld – bushland. That is how they like to fight, because they have more men and more guns than us, and it is easy for them to kill us,' he continues. 'Our ancestors and we have been on this land for much longer than the British, and we will be here for many more years after them. We must be patient. We have to think of a different way to fight them. Tomorrow, when the sun rises, we will talk about new ways to beat the British in war.'

As the sun rises the next morning, smoke swirls in a spiral towards the sky, *through the rays that stream through the trees. Chief Maqoma sits on the same rock. Ten men sit in a semicircle in front of him.*

'The British are looking for us. Their search parties are small, usually eight or twelve men. The bush is very dense, which will make it easier for us to hide and attack them by surprise. We don't wear red uniforms!'

That last statement sets off a reel of laughter from his men.

'Even when they come with many soldiers,' he continues, 'with their heavy uniforms, water bottles, packs of food and big boots, they will find it difficult to get to us up the steep cliffs and through the heavy bush. We will carry only guns, the ones we bought from the white traders, and assegais. We will smear our bodies with fat to keep warm, and if caught, we can easily slip loose from them.'

'Chief Maqoma, there are many thousands of them, and only a few hundred of us. Who will come to help us?' inquires one of the men.

'Many more Xhosa warriors will be coming soon from the Amatola Mountains and Willem Uithaaler and his Khoikhoi warriors from the Kat River will be joining us too. As you know, his Khoikhoi warriors can shoot very straight with the gun. Much straighter than we can!' he says jovially.

They all laugh again, but they all know that this strategy is new, and they do not know whether they will be more likely to live or die.

7

> Tens of thousands
> Are not enough years
> Against the barrels of guns

The same dawn that breaks over that neat little town Fort Beaufort, breaks over Newtown, a shantytown, less than a few hundred yards across the Kat River to the west, and on the way to Katberg via the Kat River Valley. About two thousand 'coloured' people live there, separate from the Xhosa people. Newtown is crowded and cramped, and has *dongas* – soil-eroded furrows – and smells of raw sewage.

*

On the way to the school hall in my dad's light blue Willys car, we bounce over the *dongas* in the road, past where Lena – the hotel kitchen housekeeper – lives.

'What are we going to do here, dad?'

'I'm going to speak to these *Hotnots* – Hottentots – about the new principal who is coming to run the school for their *kinders* – children.'

'Why is it such a small school?'

'Because not many of them bother to send their kids to school, since they're drunk all the time and it's only a primary school.'

'Do they buy their wine and sherry at our hotel to get drunk?'

'Yes. And that's enough questions from you.'

We get out of the car and walk through the main door into the school.

'*Goeie môre* – Good morning, Master, how nice of you to come. Come in and have a nice cup of tea,' says an old coloured woman with no teeth and a big smile.

We sit in a cold room the size of one of our lounges at the hotel, and it smells of cigarettes and piss. It reminds me of the lounge on the morning after Baas Bob had fallen asleep in 'his' chair and pissed his pants. It is cold. The wind is coming through broken panes of glass in the windows. There are about twenty old chairs with metal frames and plastic seats, many of them cracked, arranged in rows. I know many of the people sitting in the chairs. There is Tollie, the cobbler, his friend Sakkie, Lena, and Katie, one of our waitresses. There are others whose names I don't know, but I know them because I had seen Michael, the 'coloured' barman, sell wine and sherry to them in the liquor shop at our hotel. From when I was very young, I would often spend time with the barmen in both the 'coloured' and 'white' bars.

'*Goeie môre, mense van Newtown* – Good morning, people of Newtown,' starts my father, standing in the front of the room with his legs apart, leaning backwards slightly, his big tummy hanging forward. He says he is very pleased to announce the arrival of the new principal of the school, and that the council has decided to spend the money to fix the broken window panes, and that they were also going to put up new posts on the Newtown rugby field.

Everyone claps. He then goes on about the divisional council and the this council and the that council. I am getting very bored and start fidgeting with the broken plastic on my chair. I see him look at me out the corner of his eye, and I stop fidgeting.

Finally he says, '*Dankie vir die koppie tee* – thank you for the cup of tea,' and we get up and everyone claps loudly.

*

For the past few days I've been wondering what resistance there was to the British establishing Fort Beaufort, a military base on Xhosa land. I am reading about an attack on Fort Beaufort led by Chief Ngxukumeshe, whom the British called Hermanus Matroos. We never learned anything about the rebellion or Chief Ngxukumeshe in history at school. We all knew about Sir Benjamin D'urban, one of the governors of the Cape in the 1800s. Durban Street in Fort Beaufort was named after him.

*

'Nébi da ge ei !gu //oa – We cannot go on like this!' A Khoikhoi man pounds his fist on the ground.

He and a friend sit in a shallow cave near the Kat River. It is a cold winter's night in 1850. A small fire casts flickering black shadows on the cave walls.

'The British will kill all of us if we don't do something. They killed so many of us four years ago in the War of the Axe.'

'It is time to join up with Ngxukumeshe. I have heard he is a clever and powerful man. He also speaks English very well and is an interpreter for the British. Like us, Ngxukumeshe is Khoikhoi, but he is also half Xhosa, and a Chief of the Jwara clan. Ngxukumeshe is at Blinkwater, a little further down the Kat River in the Kat River Valley where he is looking for men to fight the British in Fort Beaufort.'

The last of the embers of the fire dies down and reduces to a tiny glow like that of a firefly.

*

Sir Benjamin D'Urban smokes his pipe in his office at the Command Headquarters overlooking Algoa Bay. He is watching the HMS Weymouth *with its three masts dock into the port. Captain Bentinck stands at attention on the other side of the desk, holding his helmet with his right arm. He looks straight ahead.*

'I disagree with you, Captain Bentinck. Hermanus Matroos is one of the finest British subjects. He is intelligent and his English is impeccable. We have a loyal ally in him against the "Kaffirs". He has shown his loyalty in his

conflicts with Chief Ngqika and Chief Maqoma. We must arm him as he has requested to keep that scoundrel Maqoma in check, and keep order among those Hottentots at the Kat River Valley Settlement,' orders the Governor. 'I believe they are becoming restless.'

*

Willem Uithaalder and Ngxukumeshe are sitting on the bank of the Kat River near the Kat River Settlement. It is late at night; all is quiet and everyone has gone to sleep. They are talking in low whispers.

'Willem, we now have many well-trained warriors – mostly Xhosa, but also some of our Khoikhoi people from the Kat River Valley,' says Ngxukumeshe confidently. 'Sir Benjamin D'Urban has sent all the weapons I requested. I said I needed them against Maqoma and us "Hotnots" in the Kat River Valley.' He chuckles softly. 'The abolition of lobola – bride price – and other Xhosa customs by that bastard Harry Smith was bad enough, but the burning of more than three hundred of our people's huts in the Kat River Valley and driving more than five hundred of them with their cattle and goats off their land is unforgivable. I will no longer fight on the side of the enemy,' he utters vehemently. 'Nési da ge a ≠omisa Fort Beaufort sa //nā-≠ams !aroma – We are now ready to attack Fort Beaufort.'

*

Dr van Tonder's consulting rooms are right next to the hotel, but he does much of his consulting in the pub, including suturing of wounds following fights. He never bothers to use local anaesthetic since most of his patients are sufficiently anaesthetised by alcohol.

I recall a story I overheard my father telling one of the customers.

One evening, while having a drink in the bar, Dr van Tonder is called to see a 'coloured' man in Newtown who was stabbed with a knife.

'Max, come with me, man. I might need a medical assistant.'

They arrive at the house made of corrugated zinc in the shantytown to find the man sitting in a chair at the kitchen table with a large laceration on the right side of his head and neck.

'*Is jy dronk, Hotnot* – Are you drunk, Hottentot?'

'*Nee, baas* – No, boss,' replies the man.

'Max, I'll need some help. Please stand behind this *Hotnot*.'

My father stands behind the man. With a swift punch to the other side of his head, the man falls unconscious into my father's arms.

'OK, Max, put him down so I can stitch him up.'

*

I am playing down at the Kat River on the Newtown side of the bridge. I see Johanna and Myrtle sitting outside their house right near the river. There is very little water in the river. It is mostly dry with deep cracks in the riverbed. It's midday and it's summer. The sweat is pouring off their faces. A cobra slithers past about a yard away from them.

'*Gee my da'i bottel bier, poesgesig* – Give me that bottle, cunt-face,' says Johanna. She sounds drunk.

'*Is nie jou bier nie, poephol* – It's not your beer, arsehole,' says Myrtle.

Sonja has a very sad look on her face. 'What has become of us "coloureds", hey? We used to be Khoikhoi. Now we say "coloureds". Now we sit with a beer bottle in our hands and fight and stab each other with knives. And we wear white people's clothes, even in summer. We don't know who the fuck we are any more!' Sonja looks at Johanna and Myrtle. '*Vok julle almal* – Fuck you all!' she shouts.

I am scared. I run back home all the way up Durban Street, across the town square to the hotel.

8

Wrong time
Wrong place
Whither the human(e) face?

Melanie and I are playing on the footpath in front of the hotel. I see something out of the corner of my eye. Suddenly I realise what it is.

'Quick, run away, there's a cobra over there!' I shout.

We all run inside the hotel.

'Mommy, Mommy, there's a snake outside,' we all scream together. We run back outside.

'Jesus wept, that's a cobra,' says my mom.

Roger Crane, who must have heard us shouting from inside the bar, sticks his head through two half-swing doors. 'Shit, that's a cobra. Everybody stand still. I'll kill the bloody thing.' He goes back into the bar and comes out with a big builder's T-square.

The cobra, about three feet long, starts to slither towards a wooden pole. That was my recollection. Melanie said she remembers the cobra being about a foot to a foot and a half at most.

Roger walks towards the snake, as if he has done this many times before. The snake stops and rears up, spreads its head wide and Roger smashes the T-square down, but just in front of it.

'Shit, missed the fuckin' thing.'

He tries again and this time gets it halfway down the body. The snake springs up into the air and lands about a yard away. He smashes it again and this time closer to the head. At first, it squirms very fast, trying to get away, but is hurt and now moves a lot more slowly. He hits it one more time on the head, and, after an even weaker wriggle, it lies lifeless. There is blood on the footpath.

'There you go, Rose. Get the Kaffir to throw it away.' Roger takes the T-square and goes back into the bar through the double half-swing doors that rattle back and forth a few times.

*

In the front of the hotel, a covered balcony spanned its entire length. The main entrance to the hotel was through two elaborately carved solid wooden arched doors flanked by stained-glass panels. The wooden pole, behind which the snake had tried to escape once, was used to secure horses while their owners had a drink in the pub. My father had the pole removed in 1964, supposedly for an extra parking space. This was an odd idea considering that Fort Beaufort, like many small towns in the area, had a main street the width of a four-lane highway. Initially the roads were made wide enough to allow for the turning circle of an ox-wagon.

*

My mom goes back to the reception office. It is on the right as you walk through the front door. On the other side of the office a staircase leads up to the second storey. It is made of dark wood, and my mom says that the railings are beautifully carved.

Outside the office, all the hotel workers are standing in line, waiting to be paid. The queue goes from the office down to the courtyard with big pots filled with flowers. My mom says they are lantana and plumbago. The plumbago has small pale turquoise flowers and sticky light-green stems. On the left side of the courtyard is the dining room; and on the right the drinking lounges. The queue goes down past the dining room, past the door to the kitchen, which one enters through a big wooden lattice arch and ends just in front of the wine cellar.

'Where was I? Who's next? Lena, three rand.'

'Please, Madam, I thought you said I could get a raise. Three rand a month is not enough to feed my family, and my husband is too sick to work now. He has heart problems, you know. *Ag* please, Madam,' says Lena with her hands held together in front of her. It looks like she is praying.

'Not this month, Lena. I haven't budgeted for a raise. Maybe next month. I'll talk to the Master about it.'

'Thank you, Madam, *dankie*, Madam,' she says, still holding her hands together in front of her.

'John the night porter. You don't do much. Here is one rand. Next.'

'Mommy, why does John the night porter get so little? He has to stay awake all night to watch the hotel.'

'Shut up and go and play. Can't you see I'm busy? It's pay day and I have to pay all the staff before lunchtime.'

I decide to go and see how my vegetables are growing. I walk past the dining hall with white cloth-covered tables to the back of the hotel and past the wine cellar and liquor storage room at the back. I carry on past the shed where the coal for the kitchen stove is kept, and the garages for guest parking. John the night porter, who sleeps in the day, has a tiny room next to the garages. Behind the garages, through a 'secret' passageway, is the 'cottage', where my grandparents, my mom's mom and dad, live. Across the road at the back of the hotel is a big piece of land with many big trees that we climb, a smaller peach tree that sometimes bears fruit, a chicken pen, a house where some of the Xhosa people who work in the hotel stay, and my vegetable garden.

I call the vegetable garden *my* vegetable garden. I'm the one who decides what should be planted, where it's to be planted, and I'm the one who watches the garden 'boy' plough the land. I help him sow the seed, push the *mielie pitte* – corn kernels – into the soil, and help water the growing plants with a hose. Every day I return to watch the little green stems rise and spiral out of the ground and grow into *mielies*, pumpkins, cucumbers, gem squash, strawberries, tomatoes, radishes, beans and watermelons. When they are ready for picking, I go to the market hall on the north side of the town square. Farmers' produce is auctioned every second Wednesday afternoon at one o'clock. Outside the hall is a large slave bell hanging between a pair of tall white-painted pillars. It's rung to mark the start of the auction and its full sound can be heard across the town square. Gibby Webster is the local auctioneer. I stand open-mouthed and amazed as I listen to how fast he can say, 'Fordee-wun, fordee-wun, fordee-wun, fordee-two, fordee-two and – one final time – fordee-two pennies to Sandy White for that box of green beans.' He slams down the hammer on the podium. I listen for the prices Gibby Webster gets for the vegetables he auctions. I then sell my vegetables to my mom for the prices Gibby gets at the auction. My mom never pays me. She says I get enough pocket money.

*

Before dawn on 7 January 1851, Ngxukumeshe is leading his troops to three strategic points around Fort Beaufort. A few days before, on the way to Fort Beaufort, he had defeated the British at Fort Armstrong and his men are ready for the next skirmish. The sun is starting to send rays of light over the hilltops covered with red aloe. He gives the order to advance.

Gunshots ring out through the still early morning heat, smoke starts to rise above the town. There is the shouting of orders and screaming of women and children. Ngxukumeshe and his twelve best warriors, all armed with British rifles, make their way across the river and up Durban Street through the smoke and chaos to the town square. There, a platoon of British soldiers stands ready, poised with their rifles cocked and pointing. Guns fire in both directions. There is first the smell of gunpowder, then the smell of blood. Bodies lie strewn and the groans and shouts of shattered bones and chests hang thickly in the air.

Ngxukumeshe lies motionless. Blood belches out of his open mouth, over his brown skin. Blood spreads over his chest and his eyes gaze vacantly into the void. Three British soldiers drag him naked across the market square and jubilantly place him under the market bell. One of the soldiers takes the Union Jack and hangs it proudly over the bell. The crowd cheers.

*

'Clang, clang, clang!' It is the end of the auction. All the produce is sold. The trestle tables are all empty and everyone is leaving.

I stand and look at the big bell just outside the market hall. I walk back to the hotel, past the courthouse, the government office building and the town hall.

9

Dongas and ditches
Open sewers
Once grass green

And that same dawn in 1954 breaks over Tini's Location, one of several townships outside of Fort Beaufort, where the Xhosa people live.

*

'Which of you kids wants to come with me to Tini's Location to see how the new school is coming on?'

'Me, me, me,' I say.

I always want to go to places with my dad. I get into our light blue Willys car. My dad drives down Campbell Street past the bowling club where my mom won the town lawn bowls championship. I don't know how, because most of the time, when I see her at the bowling club, I see her sitting with a gin and tonic in her hand rather than a bowling ball. We drive past the police station, Baas Bob's house and out on the open road towards East London. The car bounces up and down on the gravel road. We turn off to Tini's Location near the SANTA TB hospital where Lydia, one of the hotel workers, had to go when she had TB, and the road becomes even worse with potholes and *dongas*.

We pass many mud huts with thatched roofs and houses made with zinc and wood. There are mimosa thorn trees, aloes and *dongas* everywhere. Xhosa women wearing colourful blankets, bead necklaces and big black headdresses walk up from the river with buckets of water on their heads, singing.

'Yuk, it smells like the honey cart here,' I say.

My dad says nothing.

We arrive at the school building, which looks nearly finished. We get out of the car. Outside the building, a woman with a bucket of water on her head and a baby wrapped in a cloth on her back, is standing, looking at us.

'*Molo. Uphi umfundisi* – Hello, where is the teacher?' asks my dad.

'*Andimazi* – I don't know,' says the woman. She looks at me, smiling, and says, '*Molo kwedini. Uphilile* – Hello, young boy. How are you?'

'*Ndiphilile, enkosi mama*– I am well, thank you,' I say quietly, looking down at my feet.

Just then a young man arrives. He is wearing an old black jacket that has a few tears in it, a white shirt with some buttons missing, long black pants that are too short and a pair of black shoes with 'laughing' soles. He and my dad start talking very fast in Xhosa. He is the schoolteacher and says to my dad that he is very pleased with the school building.

*

When I was young, we called Tini's Location Tinis, as if it were just another meaningless name. We had no idea that the Xhosa township was named after Xhosa Chief Tini Maqoma. In fact, I did not know of the existence of Chief Tini Maqoma until I started reading up on local Fort Beaufort history.

*

It is a hot day summer's day in 1877. Dust is blown around in ascending spirals.

Chief Tini Maqoma, son of the renowned Ngqika Chief of the amaRarabe Kingdom, Jongumsobomvu Maqoma, sits outside his hut next to his brother, Ngaka, smoking a pipe. He has just bought two farms near Fort Beaufort. 'Ngaka. I don't want to make any trouble. I don't want to be imprisoned and die on Robben Island, like our father. I can at a moment's notice assemble a thousand warriors to fight the British, but I would rather live in peace and graze my cattle and grow my crops. It has become hard enough to grow food, and my cattle are starting to die from this drought.

*

'Reverend van Rooy, I am very worried. There are Mfengu employed as police patrolling my farms, and my men tell me that the British commander in Fort Beaufort plans to arrest me and send me to Robben Island to die like my father did, four years ago.

'No, no, no, Chief Maqoma. That certainly is not true,' reassures Reverend van Rooy. 'And please do come and visit me at my mission whenever it so pleases you.'

*

'That was an excellent move, Chalmers, to employ Mfengu police to patrol Maqoma's farms. I'm sure that would be most irritating to Maqoma. The Xhosa and the Mfengu, the group that fled the rule of Shaka the Zulu up north, have never seen eye to eye. On the other hand, the Mfengu have always been happy to side with us against the Xhosa tribes, for a few favours, of course,' says Holland, looking very pleased.

'Thank you, sir. I have mentioned to Sprigg that it would be better for the Fort Beaufort district if the black-owned farms were to be bought and sold to Europeans, even if that means some bloodshed. It will entail arresting and sentencing Maqoma. I'm sure we can provoke a few incidents that will allow us to charge him with sedition, sir,' says Chalmers.

*

'Ngaka, one of our men is being charged with cattle theft again. I have to go to court to testify. I am concerned that we will be attacked. I will take two hundred armed warriors with me to court in case I have to defend us.'

'A wise precaution, Tini, my brother.'

*

'Merriman,' says Chalmers, 'did you read in the Fort Beaufort Advocate *of that act of insolence and provocation – Maqoma taking two hundred of his men, armed, to a court case?*'

'Yes, Chalmers, and Holland also received an anonymous report that Maqoma is assembling his troops in the Waterkloof, just as his father did, and intends to either capture cattle – you are aware of the current food shortage – or launch an attack on Fort Beaufort. Inspector Booth also informs me that Maqoma refuses to return stolen cattle. He also claims to be the government of the area and is openly refusing to recognise us as the government. Furthermore, he later returned with a hundred armed men to Booth's station and ordered the police to leave or be killed,' reports Merriman.

'An insolent Kaffir, indeed, sir.'

'Booth did say that he was a bit drunk on that occasion, and I know that he did apologise for that incident to you, Chalmers, but I agree with your report recommending Maqoma surrender completely and disarm, or be forced to do so. I have telegraphed Holland to issue a warrant for Maqoma's arrest on grounds of sedition.'

*

'What brings you here today, Mr Groundbottom? My men's rent is not due for another two weeks,' enquires Maqoma.

'Chief Maqoma, I come early for my rent because I have heard – do not tell anyone I have mentioned this to you. I am only interested in getting my rental money, that's all – there is a warrant out for your arrest, and I believe this will happen next week. So, I just wanted to make sure I get my rental money,' replies Groundbottom nervously.

'Thank you, Mr Groundbottom. You will be paid your rent. Yes, most certainly, you will receive your rent.

*

Groundbotttom is sitting in the alehouse opposite the town hall in Fort Beaufort.

'Groundbottom, did you hear what happened to the chief whose men pay you rent?'

'No, do tell.'

'He was tried in King William's Town for high treason on six counts. All were dropped but one. He should have been sentenced to death, but some of the Fort Beaufort townspeople submitted two petitions claiming that the Kaffir wanted to live in peace, and fought back only when provoked by the government troops. So, to cut a long story short, he got life imprisonment on Robben Island, like his father. But do hear this. It is rumoured that those on Robben Island will be granted amnesty, including Chief Maqoma and that trouble-maker, Gungubele. You should be happy, Groundbottom. You'll get your rent again!'

*

The next time I go to Tini's Location with my dad, we go to another building that has a big bell outside, which somebody rings by pulling a long rope. Many people arrive and when they all sit down, my dad stands in the front and speaks to them in Xhosa. At the end they all clap and then we leave. My dad says that it was a town meeting in the community hall he had built. I know my dad didn't build it. I had seen all the 'black' labourers building it.

10

Loving but sad
Nothing bad
How cruel the hand dealt

We call our mom 'the Queen'. I am not quite sure why, but it sticks. The Queen sits and puffs on her cigarette she smokes through a small black cigarette holder. She says it removes the tar. Her thumb, second and third fingers of the left hand are a yellow-orange colour. A dark yellow streak from the smoke has coloured her grey hair on the left side. My mom smokes about eighty cigarettes a day, using a match to light each one right after she has put out the old stub. She has been smoking since she was fourteen. She says my dad's a light smoker. He only smokes about fifty a day.

*

That was my recollection. My sister claimed that our father only smoked about fifteen a day. She recalled Rose saying that Max's expectation for her to cut down her smoking to his quantity, when he only smoked fifteen a day, was unfair. Rose said it would have been fairer if he'd cut down his alcohol intake to her level. She only had a few gin and tonics a day.

*

My mom also has diabetes, which started after the birth of my brother when she was only twenty-eight. She has to inject herself with insulin twice a day, every day.

'Now what have I had to eat today?' I hear the Queen say to herself. 'I had some cheesecake at morning tea – couldn't resist – and cold meats and salad for lunch, a couple of gin and tonics, maybe more than a couple, and the usual dinner. So, how much insulin this evening? Maybe, let's say about sixty units. What are you looking at, Garth?'

'Nothing, Mom.'

The Queen opens a little black plastic box. Inside the box is a glass syringe and a dirty tissue with hardened and crusted bits of old insulin and blood on it. She wipes the needle of the syringe with the dirty old tissue, sticks the needle into her insulin bottle and sucks up some insulin into the syringe. She pulls up her blouse, puts the needle against her stomach, and presses two little metal bits on the syringe, and the needle shoots through the skin. She injects the insulin.

'Doesn't that hurt?'

'Not any more. I'm used to it.'

When the tissue becomes too dirty or crusty with insulin and little bits of clotted blood, she changes it. She never cleans the syringe, and only when the needle becomes too blunt does she change the needle.

*

When I learned about infection control at medical school, I was horrified at my mother's lack thereof with her injection technique. I sent her boxes of disposable syringes. She immediately sent them back with a note saying, 'Thanks, but no thanks. They're too much trouble, and you might have noticed that I've never had an infection at the injection sites!'

*

I know very little also of my mother's life before she had my siblings and me. She was born to Philip and Tilly Cooper in an even smaller town in the Eastern Cape called Peddie, about fifty miles from Fort Beaufort, but spent most of her childhood in a tiny hamlet called Bell. Bell consisted of my grandparents' inn and a trading store. It was between Peddie and a small seaside town called Hamburg. Peddie used to be called Fort Peddie, and was actively involved in the Eighth War of Dispossession. My mother studied bookkeeping at a technical college in Johannesburg and taught that subject at the technical college in East London.

I remember the Queen as being pretty level-headed most of the time. However, she also had a fiery temper that dissipated as fast as it arose. After her blow-ups, she would carry on as if nothing unusual had occurred, while my brother and I, who were sometimes on the receiving end, would still be shivering and shaking with fright, long after she had calmed down.

'She's temperamental, your mother – half temper, half mental,' my father said after one of her blow-ups.

My mother was slightly built, and had a thick head of hair brushed back. She walked slowly and talked slowly, except when she had one of her tantrums. I don't recall her ever running. She wore low-heeled shoes and fashionable dresses, most of which she bought from Audrey Delponte's clothes shop next to Millard's Hardware. Audrey, who came to Fort Beaufort from Port Elizabeth a few years before, was one of her best friends. They both smoked like chimneys.

Most of my recollections of her are as a depressed person. I recall rarely seeing her happy. She did all the physical disciplining in the family. When one of us was 'naughty', which meant one of us did something that made her angry, she was the one who would get the hairbrush and smack us on the buttocks – usually in a rage. We cried.

11

In nomini patris
Incense and chain
I learn by the cane

Fort Beaufort had two schools for 'white' children only. My recollection is that there was one school in Newtown for the 'coloured' kids, and one in Tini's location for Xhosa kids. The Fort Beaufort High School accepted children from Sub A to Matric. In large letters on the front wall the words 'Fort Beaufort Hoerskool' were very prominent. My dad said, 'Only in Fort Beaufort would they forget to put the two dots on top of the "o" – so our kids go to the Fort Beaufort *Whore* School!'

It was difficult to attract good teachers to Fort Beaufort. The convent school was probably no better, but my father liked the Mother Superior, so I was sent to the Convent of the Sacred Heart. I also had a friend named Michael de Wet who was a year older than me and was starting at the convent and I wanted to go to school with him. I was four years old. However, when winter arrived, I didn't want to get out of bed when it was still dark and cold and missed about three months of school. Because of this I had to repeat Sub A.

I was quite happy to go to the convent school because it meant that I got not only all the public holidays and Jewish holidays, but also the Catholic holidays. The school building itself looked a bit like a church, painted white and with pointed Gothic gables. Next to the school was the Roman Catholic church, also painted white. It had elaborate stained-glass windows depicting religious scenes. Outside the church was a large bell. It was used for the church services, and also to mark the beginning and end of each class period.

I loved the morning Masses, the chanting, the priest's elaborate white robes with gold braids and the incense burner swinging back and forth billowing fragrant white smoke.

My mother said, 'He's either going to be a bloody Catholic priest or a rabbi. My grandfather was a lay rabbi!'

On those scorching hot days in summer, with Jesus on the cross in the background, the chanting and the smell of incense, I often used to drift into a daydream that took me to other worlds, until I would be jolted back to reality by the loud clang of the bell marking the end of the service.

*

'Our father, who art in heaven, Hallowed be thy name, mumble, mumble, mumble…'

'Garth, stop mumbling and say "Our Father" properly!' blurts out Sister Maria.

'I don't know the "Our Father" yet, Sister Maria.'

'Well, pay attention and learn it!'

*

I pretty soon learned the words since we had to say the 'Our Father' at the beginning and end of every lesson.

All the teachers at the school were nuns of a German order. Most of the nuns were even stricter and more severe than the teachers at the local government school. The nuns caned us regularly for the most trivial of infringements.

One of them, Sister Walfredus, was about six feet tall and appeared to be just skin and bones under her habit. She looked ancient. She had a wizened, pale face and was one of the kinder nuns. One day a gale was blowing. Sister Walfredus was walking from the chapel back to the school building during first recess. A particularly strong gust of wind swept down the walkway. Sister Walfredus became a flying nun. The wind filled up her habit like a sail, lifted her fragile body off the ground into the air, and she flew backwards about three yards and landed on her back. My friends and I, of course, thought this was the funniest show since the clown act of the Boswell Wilkie Circus that came to town every year. Sister Walfredus fractured her right hip, a few ribs and a couple of vertebrae.

*

I have to be in the school play. I am a butterfly in *Little Jack Horner*. I don't want to be a butterfly, but I have to. The only part of the school play I like is when Ursula van der Decken finds Jack and says, 'Ah fyound him, ah fyound him end ah fyound his horn too.' When the parents come to watch, everyone laughs when she says that. The Queen says Ursula has the worst Fort Beaufort accent.

*

My mum's friend, Mrs Newell, has a kid in my class. Mrs Newell used to be a ballet dancer, and teaches ballet in the assembly hall after school. I go to ballet with my little brown moccasin slippers and learn to do first, second, third and fourth positions.

One day, Michael de Wet says to me, 'Only sissies do ballet, Garth. Don't you know that?'

That is my last ballet class.

*

It is February and my dad says today is going to be another scorcher – maybe a hundred and ten Fahrenheit.

The last class of the day is maths. Maths is my favourite subject, especially when it is at the end of the day, and especially when it is very hot. I don't know why, but when it is very hot I get drowsy and then I like adding, subtracting, dividing and multiplying.

Suddenly the bell rings. For a moment I look around to see where

I am. I see my friends in class. I pack up my books in my little brown satchel. We all stand up.

'Our father who art in heaven…'

*

I spent five years at the Convent of the Sacred Heart. When I reached Standard Three, my parents sent me to the Fort Beaufort Primary School at the other end of Durban Street, near the mental hospital, for a year. I do not recall why.

W. Austin: Fort Beaufort, 1862.

T.W. Bowler: Fort Beaufort, 1864.

Martello tower with soldier, late 1800s.

Market Square, around later 1800s.

Victoria Bridge across the Kat River.

The Grove, early Fort Beaufort.

Railway station, early 1900s.

Emgwenyeni Flats, from where the axe was stolen that sparked the War of the Axe.

Savoy Hotel, 1953.

Deane's Hotel, early 1970s.

Convent of the Sacred Heart, my first school.

The author, Neil holding his two daughters Amelie and Sofia, Melanie in front of the rebuilt Deane's Hotel site, 2010.

Artefacts from Mr Aylesbury's blacksmith in the Fort Beaufort Museum.

The author taking a photo of San artefacts from the region in the Fort Beaufort Museum.

Contemporary Fort Beaufort from the south.

12

The love of a mother
And a surrogate child
It's not black and white

Beauty Baardman was my other mother. She nurtured me probably more than did my own mother. Beauty was a Xhosa woman, but with a surname like Baardman, she may have married a man of Khoikhoi descent. The Khoikhoi descendants more often adopted Afrikaner surnames, assigned to them while working for Afrikaner farmers. The Xhosas often adopted English first names, in addition to their Xhosa first names, but kept their Xhosa surnames.

*

School holidays are over. I get my little brown satchel with my school books and put it on my back.

Beauty stomps into our bedroom. 'Let us bugga off.'

Beauty takes my hand and we walk to school across Campbell Street, past the War Memorial and Fort Beaufort museum, which we often visit to look at old guns, assegais and soldiers' uniforms, and down the hill to the Convent of the Sacred Heart on Durban Street. The Savoy Hotel is diagonally opposite the convent.

I look forward to the last school bell of the day because I know Beauty will be back to take me home, and will say again, 'OK, let us bugga off.'

The next morning I wake up with small itchy blisters on my face and my chest.

'Oh shit, you have chickenpox,' says my mom, looking at my blisters. 'Let's put some calamine lotion on. That will help the itch.'

Soon after, Beauty arrives. 'What's thet rubbish on yoh face, Toto?'

'It's calamine lotion. I have chickenpox. The Madam says I can't go to school today.'

'If you want to get rid of the chickenpox, we have to go outside and dig a hole in the ground and you must say "*Huh, huh, qiligwena*" into the hole. That will chase away the chickenpox and send it to the rich man's cattle.'

'But, Beauty, the Madam said I have to stay in bed. I'm not allowed to go outside.'

'We will have to make a hole in the room then.'

Beauty leaves the room and comes back a few minutes later with a big screwdriver. She goes to the corner of the room and with the screwdriver lifts up a piece of floorboard.

'OK. Get out of bed and shout into the hole, "H*uh, huh, qiligwena, huh, huh, qiligwena.*"'

I jump out of bed and shout as loud as I can, 'H*uh, huh, qiligwena, huh, huh, qiligwena, huh, huh, qiligwena.*'

'OK, *lungile*, that's enough.'

Within a few days my chickenpox becomes all scabs, and within a week I am better. I wonder whose cattle got chickenpox. I hope it is Bull Knott's cattle because he won't let us go *paling* – eel-fishing – on his farm, and I know he is very rich. My dad says so.

*

I think of Beauty's concept of disease and how superstitions, myths and beliefs have influenced illness and health of all cultures. I am reading a book on the San, *The Broken String: The Last Words of an Extinct People*, which has many stories of San myths and legends.

*

On an autumn day, in about 3000 BCE, finally all is quiet and the night is nearly over. A faint light begins to appear on the horizon. A young San mother is sitting cross-legged on the ground on a hill, surrounded by river except to the north, with her baby cradled in her arm and breastfeeding. Her husband is squatting next to them quietly with his bow and kudu-hide satchel of arrows by his side. Her mother is tending to the fire.

'If you see a shooting star falling in the sky, you must squeeze the milk out of your breasts and not feed it to your baby,' says her mother earnestly. 'If the baby drinks that milk, a breath of fire from the star will burn a mark on her heart. The sparks coming off the falling star are the star's lice and they can kill your baby's heart.'

The sky is clear and filled with stars.

13

> Chocolate, tin and clay
> Are the town and country
> Of children's play

It is my seventh birthday. I look at the miniature train set made of cake, and icing – white icing, red icing, green icing, blue icing, yellow icing and little silver balls.

'Look at the *Nagaapie* – bushbaby. His eyes couldn't be bigger, if he tried,' I hear my mom say.

The train has a steam engine and many carriages, and is placed on rails and sleepers. The engine is black and decorated with white and silver icing, while the carriages are all different colours, some carrying black coal, others with miniature animals inside and a few with miniature people.

'Isn't that clever?' says my mom. 'The animals and people are made of marzipan, and the people have marzipan clothes.'

There are also chocolate éclairs in the shape of small mice with shiny little silver balls for eyes.

*

Although that train cake still sticks in my mind to this day, at the time I was more interested in running around and stuffing my face with jelly and sweets than appreciating the work of art. The town baker, I think, used to use my birthdays as an occasion to express his artistic talents, which were of show-winning quality.

I don't recall seeing such artistic expression at my friends' birthday parties. Did my parents pay more, was the baker a special friend of my parents, or was it because my father was mayor of the town?

*

I get Dinky toy cars, miniature farm tractors and ploughs with all my birthdays. All my friends get them too. My mom says they are the best toys for us because they are made very strong and we can't break them easily. I have few other toys. I spend many hours with my friends playing with Dinky toys. We make whole towns and farms with roads and rivers and mountains in the soil of our backyards. We also spend a lot of time driving around the roads, ploughing the fields and bulldozing mounds.

But my favourite toys are bits of junk that I get from the scrapyard. I collect bits of metal, ball bearings from motorcars, brake shoes, spark plugs, pieces of broken gears, clutch plates, valves and other parts from car engines.

Neil and I keep all our junk in shoeboxes, which we call our junk boxes. No one else is allowed to touch them, especially Melanie. We spend a lot of time comparing our junk, or taking apart the bits of engine, or making our own toys using all our bits and pieces.

14

> The kudu knows the games
> Of rivers and caves
> Through timeless eyes of children

After breakfast I decide to call some of my friends to come and play. The telephone is black and looks a little like a Volkswagen Beetle car.

I pick up the heavy black receiver and turn the handle on the side. 'Hello, exchange, this is 63, can you please put me through to number 44.'

'*Ag*, yes of course, Garthie. Are you going to play with Johnny Reebein again, hey, *die magistraat se kleintjie* – the magistrate's little boy?' says the voice at the exchange.

'*Ja.*'

There are usually six or eight of us kids who play together – boys and girls. We often go down to the Kat or Brak River and swim or play cowboys and Indians.

A big weir across the river, not too far from the town swimming pool, is called the barrage. Sometimes we see snakes and big lizards called *likkewaans* at the river, especially around the barrage. We usually see them just above it where the water is dammed and deeper. They can swim, and we are scared of them. My dad says we must watch out for *likkewaans* because they can grow as big as me. *Oom* Hendrik says that *likkewaans* are like Australian goannas, and if one hits you with its tail, it can break your leg. When there is water in the river, we catch mullet and carp with a throw-net. My dad has a throw-net about six feet wide. I can throw the net in a perfect circle, so that it lands flat on the water spinning, and traps the fish as it sinks down to the bottom. Sometimes the net is so full of fish, my dad has to help me pull it in.

Six of my friends come to the hotel – Debbie Wolffhart and Pammie Gottlieb, who are my two girlfriends; Dessie Webster, whose Dad does the auctions at the market; Koos Wessels, who we call Fathead, because he has a big head; Johnny Reebein; and Leon Labuschagne, whose mom said she wanted South Africa to become a republic. 'If we don't become a republic, those bloody *Rooinekke*, those stupid English-speaking whities, will have us drinking next to a Kaffir in the bar. You wouldn't want that, would you?' she asked.

'Let's go down to the river and play cowboys and Indians,' says Neil.

We all head off to the river, including Melanie. We put on whatever cowboy and Indian costumes we have. We have toy guns and gun belts around our waists. Neil has a Gene Autry cowboy outfit on. I like that even more than my Davy Crockett cowboy suit. We walk down Campbell Street past Pammie Gottlieb's dad's sweet and ice cream shop. Pammie, Debbie and I often help ourselves to our favourite fizzy drink, Hubbly Bubbly, at the hotel, then go to the café and get sweets. The Queen says I will rot my teeth, but she doesn't stop us.

We take the short cut to the river, turning left at Millard's, down a small alleyway past Tollie Abraham's cobbler shop, Mr Aylesbury's blacksmith with furnace blazing and bellows, then down the hill to the river.

One day when it's raining heavily, the Queen says there's been a cloudburst. I've never seen a cloud burst open. The river is flowing strongly and has a dark muddy colour – 'Good for catching eels, Garthie,' *Oom* Hendrik always says.

'Let's run across the swing bridge,' I shout.

We run across, missing the broken wooden slats, and the swing bridge rocks back and forth.

'I want to go and play in the cave,' says Melanie.

'Do you mean the one where we've seen that sticky white stuff on spider webs?'

'What is the sticky white stuff?'

'I don't know. Joy Begbee says teenage boys go into that cave and do "stuff".'

'Oh.'

We run down the riverbank to a cave in a steep part of the bank on the eastern side of the river, about twelve feet above the water level and big enough for all of us. We have to stoop a little. The sun's rays are shining on the back wall of the cave.

'What do you think that looks like?' says Melanie, pointing to the back wall.

'Looks like a huge buck with twisted horns to me, maybe a kudu,' says Neil.

I look at the few dark lines on a large stone stuck in the hard clay wall of the cave, which could be the outline of a kudu. '*Ja*, I think so.'

*

When I was a child, I had no knowledge or consciousness of the San having inhabited the Fort Beaufort region. I have since learned that a San cave exists near the cheese factory at Kroomie, between Fort Beaufort and Adelaide and only twelve miles from Fort Beaufort. Numerous San paintings have also been found in the Katberg mountains only twenty-four miles away. We visited the Katberg mountains numerous times with my parents, and I don't recall any reference to the San or their paintings over there.

*

About 2000 BCE, upon a hill surrounded by river except to the north, stands !Xo. She is !gi:xa – witchdoctor – of her San clan. The clan is preparing for a dance. !Xo always dances first. The witchdoctor always does. !Xo dances and stamps her feet on the ground in small steps, round and round in a circle, until she is in a trance, and cold blood squirts out of her nose and she falls to the ground, her whole body shaking and twitching and shouting words no one can understand.

!Nanni must now make a painting in a cave. Sometimes !Xo does the painting, but not this time. She is now sleeping on the ground. !Nanni picks up a brown stone, takes it to the rocks nearby where there are round holes that had been made in the rock by grinding the brown stone in it many times, for many full moons.

He takes the stone and turns it round and round in the hole and makes some red powder. He then adds a few drops of water, spits into the hole, pours in a little blood from a pouch and stirs it until it becomes a smooth thick red liquid. He has many pouches on a belt around his waist. Some have stones, one has blood, another has fat and one long one has sticks with fine hairs on the one end. He walks along the eastern bank of the river to a cave on a steep slope. It is a small cave and cool inside. It has hard clay walls and part of the wall is cold rock. He takes a thin stick with some hairs from a kudu tied to the end, dips it into the red paint and very carefully and steadily draws a kudu with its long horns on the rock. He can now go to sleep. A small child squats nearby, eyes wide open. He sees it all.

*

As we grow older, the nature of our games changes. When I'm about eight years old, our favourite game is Strip Donkey. It's one of those kids' card games, where one picks up cards and the person who gets the donkey is 'donkey'. However, we create a variation. Whoever gets the donkey has to remove an item of clothing. This continues until we're all stripped naked. We don't want our parents to find out so we go into the hotel's main common shower room and lock ourselves in. As each one strips, the rest do a thorough inspection of their genitalia, and usually make a few comments, despite the fact that we have often bathed together, swum naked together in the river and known precisely what each other looked like from top to toe.

*

'Aw look, Johnny's got the root,' screams Marjory and everyone turns to stare at Johnny's erect penis, and starts giggling.

Johnny just sits with a sheepish smile on his face.

'Can you put it inside mine? My sister's boyfriend does that to my sister,' says Joy.

'How old is your sister?'

'Seventeen.'

'*Ag*, no, *sies* – yuk,' says Johnny.

*

To my knowledge, my parents never found out about this particular activity. We all knew about sex at that age, or our version thereof. In a small town surrounded by farms, we often observed dogs, chickens, cattle and sheep mating, and had a pretty good idea about what humans did as well. There were frequently stories about teenage boys who got their girlfriends pregnant. However, there was one fact we did not quite get right. We believed fertility was not age-related and that sex between six-year-olds could result in pregnancy.

*

'Hey, Garth, are you hungry?' asks my friend Andrew van Skalkwyk. He doesn't wait for me to answer. 'Let's go to the garden, man.'

Andrew lives on a farm outside Fort Beaufort. Perhaps he knows of a tree with ripe fruit or something. He leads me to a spot where there is very rich damp soil and starts digging with his hands. He quickly pulls out of the soil a few long, fat earthworms. We usually use those earthworms as bait for catching eels.

'Van, do you eat these worms?'

'Yes, they're yummy,' he says with a big smile on his face. 'I'll have yours too if you don't want them.'

*

'Hey, Mom, do you know Andrew van Skalkwyk, my new friend?' I say to my mom during lunch.

'Is he related to the van Skalkwyks who own a farm outside Fort Beaufort?'

'Yes, that's him. Do you know he eats earthworms?'

'No, but I do know his mother had German measles when she was pregnant with him and that can make the child retarded. His uncle is spastic. I don't know what caused that.'

'Is Andrew retarded then?'

'Probably.' She takes another puff of her cigarette and blows a huge cloud of smoke into the air.

*

My friend Koos Wessels is taller than me, has straight dark brown hair, and pale skin with a few freckles. Koos walks with a slight stoop and never gets angry. We are good friends and play together most days. We play cowboys and crooks, and when we are with our friends we are usually on the same side – either both 'goodies' or both 'baddies'. We go to movies together and afterwards act out the spaghetti westerns and Elvis Presley movies.

Then our parents send us to boarding school when we are about nine. I go to Selbourne in East London and he goes to Dale in King Williams Town, thirty-two miles apart. The two schools are big rivals and when we play rugby against each other, Koos and I don't talk to each other. Even during holidays we don't play together, until the middle of high school, when we forget about our school rivalry and become friends again. We never even speak about that period, as if it never happened.

15

> Lighting fires, compass and badge
> Soon ready for guns, for blood
> Baden Powell's little Boy Cub

'Ah key la, Ah key la, Ah key la, we'll do our best. We'll dib, dib, dib. We'll dob, dob, dob,' we shout at the top of our voices in the cub hall just near Mr Aylesbury's blacksmith shop.

We are standing in four straight lines dressed in our cub clothes – a green cap with yellow stripes and the Fort Beaufort Cub pack emblem badge, a khaki shirt with badges sewn on the sleeves, khaki short pants, khaki socks with a little velvet-coloured square sticking out from under the fold at the top of the sock and brown polished shoes. I am leader of the Blue Wolf Cub Pack.

We play games in the hall. The hall is also used for fetes, when it is filled with trestle tables of *melkterte, koeksusters* – custard tarts, plaited sweet pastries – and other delicious food. All the people in the town and the farmers come to fetes. No black people and coloureds are allowed. A few times a year the hall is used for teenage bops, where they dance to the local band – Mum Doodle and the Kraansburgers.

Mr Thomas is Akela (leader of the Cubs). He is almost bald, speaks with a poncy English accent and walks with a very straight back. We say he has a carrot up his arse. He has taught us how to light fires and how to survive in the veld. Making fires is everyone's favourite activity. There are few Afrikaner children in Cubs. They have their own group called Voortrekkers. We don't like them, but when they aren't at Voortrekkers, many of them are our friends and we play together.

'We are going to have another survival day in the veld, boys. Tell your parents you all have to be here at eight o'clock on Sunday morning,' says Mr Thomas. 'I want everyone in full Cub uniform. Bring a bottle of water, matches to light a fire and a compass.'

Sunday morning eight o'clock, it is already hot. Mr Thomas says it is going to be a scorcher. We all pack into a few parents' Kombis and drive past the airport and halfway to Healdtown.

'Now, boys, get into your packs – Yellow Pack there, next Blue Pack, then the Red Pack, and over there the Green Pack. We're going to learn how to find your way in the veld. Pack leaders pick up your set of instructions over there. You'll use those instructions, your compass and common sense to get to a special meeting point. Each pack will get there by a different route. It will take you about two hours to find the spot. And remember – don't try to play with snakes if you see any. Now off you go.'

As leader of my pack, I have the instructions. 'It says walk east fifty yards to a large mimosa tree and look there for your next clue. Let's go! Come on, Koos. You don't want to get lost, do you?'

We feel like loyal scouts to Baden Powell, learning the skills to help the British fight the Afrikaners in the Boer War. On rainy days, Mr Thomas reads all the stories about Baden Powell to us in the cub hall. Through these stories we learn what a hero he was, and all about how he started Cubs and Scouts. We also like to think of ourselves as Mowgli, who was brought up by wolves in the jungles of India and was able to survive by tracking and hunting.

*

The tracking and hunting skills of the local San and Khoikhoi in the desert and semi-desert of our own region never entered our consciousness, nor that of anyone else in the town.

*

We run to the mimosa tree full of sharp white thorns that look like bull's horns. We walk around, looking for the next clue. Alan McComb picks a thorn off the tree and sticks it into Michael Minty's bum.

'Ow, you little shit. I'll bash you.'

The rest of us laugh and giggle. Michael is cross.

'Don't do that,' I say. 'If Mr Thomas finds out, you know what will happen. Our whole pack will be punished and we won't get our survival badge. There's a stone with a piece of paper under it.'

Koos grabs it and reads. 'Two hundred yards ten degrees north-west. Hint – you should find yourself on top of a *koppie* – hillock.'

We get out our compasses.

'That's that way. But look, there are three *koppies* over there.'

'Keep your compasses on ten north-west and let's walk,' I say.

We haven't gone more than twenty yards when James screams, 'There's a *rinkhals*. Let's chase it.'

'Idiot, no! Didn't you hear what Mr Thomas said?' I am more worried about getting into trouble and not getting my survival badge than about James being bitten by the snake.

The sun is getting hotter and there is no shade other than under mimosa trees and other small shrubs. We get to the top of the *koppie*. Under another stone is a note – 'Look for the smoke signal to your south-west and follow it for five hundred yards.'

'Aw, that's not fair. One of the other packs got to light a fire. Where is south-west?'

'Look at the sun or your compass and figure it out, fool.'

Koos looks at the sun and points. 'That's south-west.'

'No, it's not, *poephol* – arsehole,' says Michael, looking at his compass. 'It's there.'

'Well, I don't see any smoke. Maybe they can't make a fire.'

'Let's just start walking south-west.'

'No, we have to wait for the smoke. We might not see it from the bottom of the *koppie*.'

'How long will we wait, then?'

We sit on top of the *koppie*, the sun beating down on us. My arms are already turning red-brown. Michael's pale skin has gone bright red. I have almost finished my water bottle.

Two hours later, we reach an open clearing where Mr Thomas, his wife and the Red Pack are sitting on the ground, eating sandwiches. The Green Pack soon arrives and dives into their sandwiches. After half an hour, still no Yellow Pack.

Mr Thomas is looking a little worried. 'Anyone seen any of the Yellow Pack?' he asks.

'No, Akela,' we shout together.

'They must be lost,' says Alan with a naughty smile on his face.

'We better form a search party,' says Mr Thomas with a frown on his forehead. 'The Yellow Pack should be coming from the south-west as well. The pack leaders come with me. The rest of you, stay put, and don't move from here.'

We go off with Mr Thomas, who is walking very fast.

I recognise the spot where we saw the *rinkhals* slithering away between the shrubs.

'Mr Thomas, maybe we should look for tracks like Mowgli does,' says Dessie. The back of his neck is burnt bright red.

All of us immediately start looking for shoe marks in the red earth.

Half an hour goes by, and still no sign of the Yellow Pack.

Mr Thomas is looking very worried. In his proper English voice he occasionally tries to shout, 'Yellow Pack, where are you?' He can't shout very loudly.

After an hour we come to a ridge. I have a feeling we will find them near here.

To my right I see a bunch of bones half-buried in the ground. I pick one up. 'Akela, look, this bone looks like a kudu leg bone. Looks just like the kudu bone we have at the hotel. *Oom* Hendrik gave it to me after he stripped it to make biltong.'

'I don't care if it is a kudu bone. Keep your mind on finding the Yellow Pack.' Mr Thomas is angry.

'I think they might be down at the dry riverbed over this ridge, Akela. I often play there with my sister, and my dad. I think I can hear them.'

The sun is about to go behind the mountains in the west.

Dessie shouts at the top of his lungs, three times louder than Mr Thomas, 'Yellow Pack, where the hell are you?'

'Here,' comes a soft voice from the direction of the dry riverbed.

Mr Thomas smiles. The frown on his forehead disappears. Over the ridge near the river bed three boys are whimpering softly, two are walking around kicking river stones and the others are sitting, just staring at the ground.

*

I have been unable to find much information on interactions between the San and the Khoikhoi, other than in history books that mention that the San were displaced from their gathering and hunting grounds into the Kalahari Desert systematically by the Khoikhoi, then the Xhosa, then the Europeans.

*

It is about 1500 BCE. A young San man, short and slim and clad only in a small kudu-skin loincloth, sits on top of a koppie *looking into the distance. He can see smoke lifting slowly into the air. He knows there are no San tribes in that direction. He has heard that there are Khoikhoi people there, living in huts made of grass, and that they keep cattle. They also hunt the deer where the San people hunt. Tonight he will go and see who these people are.*

With a bow and a pouch of arrows hanging over his right shoulder, he sets off in a south-westerly direction. He tramps so lightly on the ground that he can barely be heard. Not even the birds give a warning signal. He can see a few fires in the distance. As he grows close, he can smell the smoke from the fires and is now crawling on his stomach. He peers over a ridge and counts twenty huts, bigger than the one he sleeps in. In the middle of the huts are ten cows surrounded by a kraal made of mimosa branches. Some people with skins covering their bodies sit in front of a fire, drinking milk from a calabash.

Hanging from a branch of a tree he can see a carcass of a deer, skinned and still dripping with fresh blood. That is one of our deer. Maybe we can take one of their cows and drink the milk, he thinks to himself. He swivels around silently on his stomach and makes his way back to his family.

*

Every year on Remembrance Day, the Moths (Members of the Tin Hats – Second World War veterans), Cubs, Brownies, Girl Guides and Scouts dress up in their uniforms to remember those who died in the First and Second World Wars, and sing hymns.

We assemble at the Cub hall at ten o'clock. This year I am leading the Cubs. I stand in front of all the Wolf Cub Packs holding a wooden wolf's head on a broom stick at forty-five degrees, with the bottom end of the stick pressing into my stomach. In front are the adults, then the Scouts and Girl Guides, and at the back the Cubs and Brownies.

Mr Thomas shouts as loudly as he can, 'Forwaaaaaard march!'

We start off all over the place, heading in different directions up Campbell Street. By the time we get to the top of the street, we are marching more or less together.

Mr Thomas shouts again as we get to the town square, 'Leeeeeft turn!'

The adults, Scouts and Girl Guides all turn left, half the Cubs and Brownies turn left, some turn to the right and some don't know what to do so just carry on straight.

'Everybody to the left, please!' Mr Thomas tries to shout.

Those off track look around and scurry more or less in the right direction.

We reach the War Memorial and stand in our packs in a square around it. We know more or less where to go because we had a rehearsal yesterday.

It is summer. Remembrance Day is always in summer and always very hot and there are always flies buzzing around our faces. In the middle is an organ from one of the churches. Every year the same old lady with grey hair in a neat little bun at the back of her head plays the organ.

First there are speeches. My dad, the mayor, always makes a speech. All the men have dark blue blazers on, white shirts, ties, long grey pants and their medals pinned to the blazer pockets. The Moths all have their Moth ties on. We don't know what the speeches are about, but they always say things like 'our fathers that begat us' – whatever 'begat' means.

At about midday, the old lady with the grey hair and the bun plays the hymn 'Oh God our help in ages past'. By then we have been standing in the 105-degree heat for about an hour, and at least three young Cubs, Brownies or Scouts have fainted. Mr Thomas rushes around with a bottle of smelling salts and puts it under their noses and slaps their cheeks to revive them. They are allowed to go and stand in the shade at the courthouse.

Two years ago, one of the Girl Guides with a long ponytail fainted. She fell backwards and her ponytail got caught on one of the spikes of the iron fence. A year later she had to go to Cape Town to have treatment for brain cancer. We were sure the spike had caused it. We now stand far away from that fence.

*

A young San man, about seven hundred years ago, comes running up to a group of men of his tribe squatting around a fire on a hill surrounded by river, except to the north. There is still mist lying low on the ground and the men have their animal skins wrapped around themselves as they chat.

'While I was tracking a big kudu, I saw my uncle. He said he met people who come from far away. They are bigger than us and keep many cattle. They speak a language very different from ours. He could not understand them, but they exchanged gifts. We must find out more about these people,' he said with some urgency in his voice.

'We will send out our best trackers to look for them.'

'What do they do with their cattle? Do they drink their milk like the Khoikhoi?'

'ǃu-ta ge a. ǂguixun ge hâ //a khoin xa da lúna, tsi da ge nî ǂûi – I don't

know. There are many things we don't know about those people, and we must find out.'

*

It is early evening. The sky is clear and there are many stars. An old woman sits in the middle of a small group, slowly and softly singing a repetitive song. A number of women around her join her in harmony.

The trackers return and sit quietly until the singing stops.

'Tare-ets go hó≠ui, //Kabbo – What have you found out, //Kabbo?'

'They call themselves Xhosa – it means "the angry people", but they seem very friendly to me. They have many cattle that they eat, and they drink their milk. I learned some of their words – molo, uphilile – hello, how are you?' said //Kabbo, looking very pleased with himself. 'I also tried to teach them a few words of our language, but they had trouble with our click sounds. I think we should invite their leaders to come at the next full moon. We can kill a deer.'

'Of course they will be very friendly if you keep giving them gifts. You would give a gift to a snake, //Kabbo. I think we must be careful,' warns the old woman.

The new moon begins to rise in the east.

16

The hunter, the hunted
The conqueror, the conquered
Who holds the snooker cue next?

I am standing with a snooker cue in my hand, peering over the snooker table, aiming to sink the blue ball. The snooker room is next to the bar. The table is full-sized and doesn't have any rips in the green felt. I don't know how it has stayed in such good condition, because most of the regulars who drink in the pub are drunk most of the time, and snooker and darts are what they play in-between drinks. I often hang out in the bar with my dad and practise my snooker and darts when not helping him serve the customers. The bar has a long counter made of shiny dark heavy teak wood.

A couple of years later, my dad has the old teak bar counter taken out and replaced with varnished split pine slats. He says he wants to modernise the pub.

Not all the customers are happy with the change.

'Max siz a fuggin idyut. Even au know teak ish fuggin valuable shit,' I hear Harry Els say once after about his eighth Lion lager.

I sink the blue ball and am about to go for the pink when a man about my dad's age, clean-shaven, with neatly combed brown hair and dressed in a light blue safari suit, walks into the bar.

'Garthie, will you serve the gentleman, please.' My dad is sitting on the customer side of the bar counter with a glass of JB whisky in his hand.

I leave my solo snooker game and serve the man. I look at him, then look at my dad. My dad hasn't shaved today, has dark stubble on his face, and is dressed in his khaki outfit with his shirt half hanging out of his short khaki pants. The shorts are tucked under his big paunch. I go back to my snooker game.

After a few drinks and a long chat with my dad, I hear the man say, 'Well, Max, very nice to have met you. I must leave now and change into something respectable. I have a meeting with the mayor at midday.'

'Goodbye,' says my father, smiling.

*

My dad is having a meeting in the front lounge of the hotel. He is always having meetings. He goes to Freemason meetings, Moth meetings, divisional council meetings, rugby club meetings, cricket club meetings and who-knows-what meetings.

We are standing outside the lounge with our ears stuck to the door, trying to hear what they are saying.

'They're singing "It's a Long Way to Tipperary",' says Melanie. She barges into the meeting, joining in the song, which we all know well.

The room is filled with a group of men dressed in dark blue blazers and Moth ties, staring at her and looking very angry.

'Melanie, I've told you before. Do not come barging into my meetings. Now get!' shouts my father.

We all run down the passage, giggling.

At another meeting of the Moths in the front lounge, I hear my dad say, 'If they come, we are ready for them.'

We don't know who they are, but we guess it is the blacks. I imagine 'them' coming over the hills in their thousands into town with assegais and shields and my dad with all those old guys (in their forties) with their cannons and guns behind sand bags and bunkers and smoke everywhere – just like I'd seen in photos in the Fort Beaufort museum of the Kaffir Wars a hundred years ago.

*

When I was at the university in Cape Town, I learned that the University of Fort Hare in Alice was an African National Congress 'hot bed'. As an adult, it dawned on me that 'they', for whom my father and his Members of the Tin Hats mates were 'ready', were presumably armed African National Congress cadres.

*

It is early evening in September 1883. The sun is setting behind the dark shadows of the mimosa thorn bushes and aloes. A group of men are squatting beside the fire in the middle of their kraal.

'*We found new ways of fighting the white man. We would attack them when the weather was cold and raining because their guns did not work as well when it was wet. Also, Maqoma was very clever. He knew we could not beat them in the open fields. So instead, he ambushed them in small groups. They did not know how to fight us like that in the forests.*'

'*So, how did you get chased off your land?*' *asks one of the younger men.*

'*Well, they learned that without food, we could not fight, so the British burned all our crops, and our women could not feed us. They also did not care how many of their men died. They just brought more and more of their soldiers, until there were just too many of them for us. More and more white people came to eBofolo. White men with big brown hats, and their wives with small white hats came with their wagons pulled by oxen. They don't speak English. They speak a different language, Afrikaans. The British call them Boers.*'

*

Besides running the hotel, Max also taught part time at a school in Healdtown. The school was originally set up by Methodist missionaries in 1845 for 'black' children, a small community about six miles from Fort Beaufort. Nelson Mandela and other political leaders such as Robert Sobukwe, Govan Mbeki and Raymond Mhlaba and a past rugby board president, Silas Nkanunu, received part of their school education at Healdtown, but not during the time my father taught there. I recall my father telling me that he found it difficult teaching 'black' children poetry about the sea when they had never seen the ocean. It occurred to me that most of the 'whites' in Fort Beaufort had also never seen the sea!

17

> Between the paths
> Hedges of Elephant grass
> Begin the destruction

In the middle of the town, next to the town hall and opposite the hotel, was a large park full of trees, flowers and hedges of elephant grass, a wily succulent with tiny round leaves. Everyone called it the Grove. In addition, the park had a children's playground with a swing and a slide, and a number of tennis courts. The English-speaking 'whites' predominantly used these courts, particularly the farmers, who used to play tennis every Sunday. Adjacent to the courts was the clubhouse, a neat white building. Inside were chairs and tables covered with starched white tablecloths. Behind a long counter was a small kitchen. Volunteers, who were the wives of the men playing tennis, or the old ladies of the town, ran the clubhouse. They served tea in china teapots covered with hand-knitted tea cosies and delicate china cups and saucers along with scones, apricot or strawberry jam and thick cream at morning and afternoon tea. At some point, the council tried to create a tropical effect by building a couple of ponds with little islands in the middle. These were planted with bamboo. Despite the arid conditions, the bamboo grew to about forty feet tall. We used to scrape the fine hairs under the leaves covering the bamboo stems and rub it down each other's backs and chests. We called it itchy powder. It produced an intense itch that lasted for hours.

*

Neil, Melanie, me and many of our friends play 'bicycle touches' in the park. Whoever is 'on' has to try to touch someone while riding on his or her bicycle. We mostly stick to the paths, but sometimes take short cuts through the elephant grass hedges, flowers and shallow goldfish ponds.

I have a Raleigh bike with a Sturmey Archer three speed. I can go a lot faster than some of my friends who don't have any gears. We arrive back home after playing bicycle touches for a couple of hours.

My dad is standing on the front veranda, looking at us. 'Garth,' he says. I know I am in trouble when he says Garth, not Garthie or Toto.

'I have had complaints that you and your friends have been destroying the park playing bicycle touches. From today, that is forbidden.'

'But where can we play bicycle touches then? The park is such fun because it has all these paths and hedges and stuff. That's not fair.'

'Listen, I am the mayor. I cannot have people complaining to me about my own children. That's final.'

'Just because you're the mayor doesn't mean you can just tell us what to do. The park belongs to everyone.'

'Don't let me catch you playing bicycle touches in the park again!'

*

My mom is sitting at her desk in the reception office, smoking a cigarette.

'Mom, what can we do?' asks Neil. 'Dad says we aren't allowed to play bicycle touches in the park any more.'

'You bloody kids make me sick. That's all you can say – what can I do, what can I do? Go, scat. Go and make something.'

Neil and I walk slowly to the back of the hotel.

Suddenly Neil gets a big smile on his face. 'Why don't we build a space rocket, Garth?'

He has a very active imagination. We had seen a sputnik in the sky the previous night. That must have given him the idea.

'Good idea. We have enough bits of metal in our junk boxes to build one.'

We sit down at a table in the courtyard and plan a three-stage rocket that we will launch from the backyard of the hotel. We had seen a picture of how they were built in Knowledge magazine that I get every month.

'Hey, Garth, when the rocket is a thousand miles into the sky, the first stage will burn out and fall off, then the second-stage engine will start and take the rocket even higher, and then circle round the Earth.'

'How will we get the rocket to land back in Fort Beaufort?'

'I don't know.'

We build the outer shell with baked beans cans and use solder and a soldering iron to fuse them together. We are pretty good at using a soldering iron, having had a lot of practice making many crystal radio sets. We use bits of metal from our junk boxes to divide the stages of the rocket. For the control panel in the capsule, we use bits of old motorcar control panels. Parts we don't have, we get from the Fort Beaufort junkyard near the high school.

The rocket is about three feet tall. At the bottom are three exhaust jets. We build the launching pad from parts of an old ironing board. Each fuel chamber is a combination of solid paraffin mixed with gunpowder that we get by emptying many firecrackers from Pammie Gottlieb's dad's café. The bottom stage of the rocket has three triangular wings to make it fly straight. It takes us about three weeks to finish building it.

'Do you think we should tell everyone to come watch the rocket launch?' asks Neil.

'Yes, good idea. Er, actually no. What if Mom and Dad won't let us, and Mom tells us we are bladdy mad? What if it doesn't take off? No, not a good idea,' is my final reply.

I take the long piece of string soaked in paraffin and feed it into the first stage. The other end I take around the corner of the building about twenty yards away. We look around to make sure that no one is looking on.

'Hey, Neil, we are rocket scientists, man!'

'*Ja.*'

I light the end of the string and the flame starts to move slowly towards the rocket. We both carefully stick our heads around the corner to see what is going to happen. The flame goes into the bottom of the first stage of the rocket.

Nothing happens.

'Let's go and have a look, Garth,' says Neil.

'No, let's wait a little longer.'

Just then there is an explosion and metal goes flying in all directions and bits of the rocket lie burning on the launching pad. I look towards the dining room wall. Bits of metal are stuck in the wall, but none has hit the windows. I see my darkly tanned skin turn pure white.

*

I don't recall my parents' reaction to this event, but Neil remembers my mother, who found out about the mishap sometime later, saying something like 'You bloody kids could have burnt down the bloody hotel.' That was pretty mild, considering the potential consequences of our unsupervised activity. I shudder when I think of the injuries we might have sustained.

*

That is not the end of Neil's space travel. He has a friend, Johan Dippenaar. His dad, Jan Dippenaar, is our family's GP. Jan took Melanie's appendix out when she was about nine. Melanie told us that when she woke up, he and my dad were having a whisky at her bedside. But that has nothing to do with Neil's space travel.

Neil and Johan like to dress up as characters from outer space with masks and colourful Superman-style capes, and run around town as aliens. They don't do too much alien – just run around the streets or play regular games in their outfits. Neil's alien name is Spunty and his friend is Mangalies. I don't understand what goes on in their heads when they run around town in those outfits.

At night Neil pretends that he, my dad and I get onto a spaceship, which flies to a planet called Eartherland. Of course, no girls are allowed, only him as Spunty, my dad as Bambus and me as Melastation. In the morning, we tell Melanie all about the fantastic time we have in Eartherland. Everything on Eartherland is bigger and better than on Earth.

*

Why we were so mean to Melanie, I am not quite sure. Maybe it was a typical boy–girl thing. Maybe it had something to do with the fact that she was a biter as a very young child. My father had told me I was not allowed to hit girls. When Melanie got angry with me, she would latch on to some part of my body with her teeth like a pit bull. Since I was not allowed to hit her, I would stand and scream until someone arrived to detach the mouthpiece from my flesh. I don't recall her biting my brother. What Neil might have had against her other than a bit of sibling rivalry as the youngest child, I am unsure.

That was not all that Melanie liked to bite. She also loved biting into chunks of raw meat. On one occasion she had sneaked a chunk of raw meat from the pantry and was eating it in the courtyard of the hotel. My mother came by and must have seen her quickly put her hand behind her back.

'What have you got there, Melanie?'

'Nothing.'

There was a sudden look of surprise and dismay on her face. Dinky, our dog, nonchalantly appeared from behind her and trotted off down the courtyard with a large chunk of raw meat in her mouth.

18

> Moskva, Telz, Vilna say some
> The mysteries bygone
> Hidden by one

It is a Sunday in September 2012 and I am in Vilnius, Lithuania. My wife Melissa and I enter the Tolerance Centre of the Vilna Goan State Jewish Museum on Naugarduko Street.

'Two tickets please,' I request, practising my rudimentary traveller's Lithuanian.

Hearing my foreign accent, the woman behind the ticket desk asks in English, 'Where are you from?'

'We're from Australia,' I reply.

She seems quite friendly and I decide to push my luck a little. 'I was born in South Africa and three of my four grandparents came from Lithuania. Do you know where I might get some information on them?'

'In fact, I do,' she replies. 'I have a friend who works at the State Archives who I'm sure will be able to help you. Look around our museum and I will give you her contact details later.'

*

When I was a teenager and became interested in my ancestry, my parents said they had never asked their parents about their lives in Lithuania and Russia and their journey to South Africa, and my grandparents' memories had faded or become distorted.

'Got, you von't believe it, but in Russia da cherries ver da size of vortermelons,' was my Granny Tzatzke's reply to my constant questioning about her life in Lithuania.

I never knew whether to believe her, because she also insisted that she came from Moscow and had visited Vienna.

'All your grandparents came from Lithuania. They left when they were teenagers, fleeing pogroms in the mid-1890s,' said my uncle Hilly Cooper.

Melanie recently found our mother's birth certificate, which stated that her parents, Tilly and Philip, were both from a town in Lithuania called Kovono.

My great aunt Betty said, 'They had to pay the border guards to get out of Lithuania and walked for days or weeks to get to the coast and board a ship. One of the teenagers decided at the last minute that he didn't want to leave and started to run back. The border guard chased him and said, "You've paid your money, now go!" and dragged him kicking and screaming by the scruff of his neck across the border to join the rest of the group.'

At that time, there were boats going mainly to South Africa and the USA. My grandparents landed in South Africa, speaking only Russian and Yiddish. Where they landed and what they did to survive initially, I have been unable to find out. There was quite a sizable Jewish Lithuanian community in South Africa. They may well have had connections with them.

Granny Tzazke married Gutel Alperstein, after whom I was named. He was also called Gutman, and they lived on a farm in Middledrift. They ran a trading store that catered for the local Xhosa community who lived in mud huts in the surrounding district, and grew tobacco on their farm. Middledrift consisted only of a post office, the trading store, a number of farms and the Xhosa community. They had four children, including my father. I recall being told by my mother that Gutel died at age seventy-six from a stroke the day before I was born. I had never considered until recently how that might have affected my father. Granny Tzatzke then moved into the hotel my parents had bought in Fort Beaufort.

*

We look around the museum and about an hour later I notice the same woman from the reception desk speaking with a young man in Russian. A month earlier we had spent a week in St Petersburg in Russia and I had learnt some Russian.

'Would you be able to give me your friend's details now?' I ask in somewhat broken Russian.

She is clearly not expecting Russian to come out of my mouth. She smiles. 'Wait. I call my friend now.'

'Please don't disturb her on a Sunday.'

'No problem.' She speaks in rapid Russian on her mobile for a few minutes, then hands me her phone. 'Talk to her.'

I greet her nervously in Russian.

'You come tomorrow morning nine o'clock. My friend, she give you my address,' she says in English with a very thick Russian accent.

The next morning I take the bus to the Lithuanian State Historical Archives to meet with the Russian Lithuanian contact who is the deputy manager of the State Archives. I stand outside a solid grey cement Soviet-looking building. Above the weathered doors of the main entrance the words *Lietuvos Valstybes Istorijos Archyvas* stand out on a dark plaque. I have with me a note with the names and possible dates and places of birth that I had collected, including from a relative who is an amateur genealogist and my aunty, Kitty Cooper. There are more questions than facts.

I ring the bell and am ushered in by an elderly man. A few older women stand around and gaze at me curiously. They seem to know why I am here. One of the women, with a smile, motions me to walk down the corridor and ushers me into an office. Behind a large desk sits a stern-looking woman who looks to be in her late fifties or early sixties.

I deliver my best, polite and lengthy Russian greeting and introduction that I had practised a number of times.

She looks at me with a bored expression, her jaw resting in her right hand. 'What do yourrr want? What inforrrrmaition do you hev?' she asks.

I go over all the information I had about my grandparents that had been collected by a relative, Roy Ogus and my aunt, Kitty Cooper, Hilly Cooper's wife. I hand her a piece of paper where I had written down all the details.

'Start with Philip Cooper, maybe not Cooper, maybe Kuper. No such place as Rosalia [his birthplace according to my aunt]. Must be Rozalimas – tiny *shtetl* – no information from there. Only nine hundred people living there today. Next Teresa, Tilly Kahn. Teresa [as recorded by my aunt] not a Jewish name, maybe Tilly yes. Born in Tels. No, not Tels, Telšiai [pronounced Telshay]. Her mother name Roselea, rubbish, not a Jewish name, and Isadore also, not Jewish names. Rubbish.'

I show her my mother's birth certificate. It is written that Philip and Tilly were born in Kovono.

'They all say that. By the way, Kovno, not Kovono – wrong spelling. Lithuania has many government districts, one of them then was Kovno, today Kaunas, and people often just mentioned the district, not the *shtetl*, some of which didn't even have names. Both Rozalimas and Telšiai were in Kovno district.'

Concerning Gutel or Gutman Alperstein, she says, 'So many *shtetls* in Vilna district, probably won't find nothing.' With regard to my father's mother she says, 'Kaila Jewish name, not Keila, and surname, yes, Sarxe [the Russian pronunciation being Sarguh – the 'g' being a gutteral 'g']. Find someone from Moscow, forget it. By the way,' she says, 'Lithuanian spelling of Alperstein is Alpershtein, and you say it Alpershtain.'

She slowly walks over to a large cream-coloured metal filing cabinet and pulls out a number of old handwritten records from the 1800s, looks at the relevant dates and variations on spelling of names and does the same on the computer for computerised records.

'Nothing. You can do an official search for Gutel Alpershtein which will cost you three hundred litas.' She then leans over towards me and says quietly, 'I have been doing this research for many, many, years and my experience tell me you will probably get nothing.' She puts both her arms out with palms facing up, and her head leaning over to one side, in a typical Jewish gesture and says, 'But if you want to spend the money, spend your money. Here is my card, just email me.'

*

We only have time to go to either Telšiai or Rozalimas for a day. Telšiai is a large town of about fifty-five thousand people, and a little further from Kaunas than Rozalimas. I do not know where to start looking for evidence of where my grandmother Tilly may have come from in Telšiai.

So we decide to go to Rozalimas. I discover there is no public transport to Rozalimas, and it's about a two-hour drive from Kaunas where we are heading to next. In Kaunas, due to my limited Lithuanian, we hire a driver named Dario. He has never heard of Rozalimas, but he types it into his GPS system, a map comes up, and off we go.

We arrive two hours later. It is a little wooded oasis in the middle of flat open plains, with a few modern houses, but mainly simple wooden houses turned grey from age, each with a small vegetable garden. It looks like a village of maybe two hundred, not nine hundred people. We approach the village square and get out of the car. There is a church from the late 1800s, just after my grandparents would have left Lithuania, and next to it a board with 'attractions' of Rozalimas, which includes a synagogue and a museum. We start walking around, trying to find the synagogue.

An elderly lady comes by on a rickety bicycle.

'Dario, can you ask her where the synagogue is and whether there are any Jewish families in town?'

Dario stops her and chats for a while. 'She says the synagogue is around the corner. Only Jewish families lived here a hundred years ago, but now there are none.'

'What happened to the Jews?'

They have another conversation.

'She says she doesn't know.'

We walk a short distance and find a building on the corner of the narrow street which fits the old lady's description and the photo on the board in the town square. It is an old wooden building like an ordinary barn, very weathered. It looks like it's about to collapse. All the windows and doors are boarded up and there are cobwebs everywhere. There is a blue plaque with a 'T' on one of the sides, but no information indicating that it is marked for restoration. It seems extraordinary but this must be the synagogue. We take photos of it. The old lady had said we might get more information from the village museum at the other end of town. We make our way to the museum.

We pass a large stone with an inscription.

'Dario, what does that say?'

'It says founded in the sixteenth century.'

We pass another church with a large well-kept cemetery around it. There are people tending the graves, which are immaculately kept. We look at headstones, but cannot find any with Jewish names or with inscriptions in Hebrew. The cemetery continues beyond a low stonewall. It is too extensive for us to search further.

We reach the museum, but it looks closed. A woman cleaning the museum informs us that the person who has the keys has just left for the day.

'They have come all the way from Australia to see the museum,' says Dario.

'OK, just wait, I call her.' She makes a call on her mobile. 'Just fifteen minutes, she will be here.'

Fifteen minutes later, a middle-aged woman comes wobbling down the road on her bicycle, and opens up for us. The museum doesn't contain any information before the mid-1900s. People from Israel, USA, South Africa and Australia have signed the guest book. Clearly, many other people had been on a similar quest.

How would Philip as a teenager have got from here to Peddie, South Africa? I wondered. When would his family have arrived here, and from where, and why?

The next day Melissa says to me, 'Your mother Rose's name on her birth certificate is Rosa Lina, isn't it? I don't think that is a coincidence.'

19

My past I hear again and again
The sound of a beat
An African drum

'Where have you bloody kids been? It's almost dark and – Jesus wept! You're all wet and full of mud.'

'We've been playing down at the river, Mom.'

'Tell Beauty to make sure you have a bath before you come down for dinner,' shouts my mom as we run up the stairs. 'And make sure she cleans behind your ears. They're always filthy.'

James Moosa beats the brass gong. It is dinnertime. James is the headwaiter. He is from Tanganyika. He speaks Swahili and thinks he is better and more important than the other waiters, who are all Xhosa. His skin colour is very black – blue-black. He is also totally bald, and his dark head is very shiny. He looks like a chief. Five minutes before each meal he puts on his red jacket, hangs a white cloth over his arm, picks up the shiny circular brass gong and gong stick, and exactly on time, walks around the courtyard of the hotel beating the gong as if he is beating an African drum, and the same African drumbeat rhythm every time.

We run downstairs, into the dining room, and sit down at the family table. My granny, my dad's mom, comes and sits with us. We order our meals.

'There's *chaza* – pork – in that, Granny,' says Neil, as we are about to start eating dinner.

'Oi Got, thenks for telling me,' says my granny in her thick Russian-Yiddish accent.

'Don't listen to him,' says Melanie. 'He's just teasing you, Granny.'
'Oh goot.' She sighs with relief.
'No, Granny, I think Neil might be right, 'I pipe in.
'Oi Got, vot must I do? Ken I eat it or not?'
'You better not, Granny,' says Neil.
'Don't listen to him, Granny,' says Melanie.
This goes on until Granny's food is cold, and she is totally confused.

My granny, whose real name is Keila, is also called Katy, but is mostly known as Granny Tzatzke. *Tzatzke*, my dad says, is the Yiddish word for trinkets and cheap jewellery.

*

The next morning after breakfast, Granny Tzatzke is baking something in the kitchen.

'Lena, gif me da flour. I also vant lots of butter ant sugar,' Granny Tzatzke orders the workers in the kitchen.

We like to watch her cook.

'What are you making today, Granny,' asks Melanie.

'*Kichlach*. Katy, bring me da baking tray.'

'Granny, you promised to make me *gehakte* herring.'

'Yes, I vill make you *gehakte* herring and gefilte fish and *kneidlach* and *gehakte lebe*, and *taichlach*, and *tsimis*. You like *tsimis*, don't you?'

'Yes, Granny, but I want *gehakte* herring.'

'OK, OK.'

Just then, Taffy, our Welsh barman, who always has brown powder on his upper lip from sniffing snuff, barges into the kitchen.

'Where is Mr Alperstein? Where is Mr Alperstein? I am looking for Mr Alperstein,' he says in his strong Welsh accent. He looks angry.

'I don't know, Taffy,' I say. 'Why?'

'George hit me on the earhole. George hit me on the earhole. I am going to tell Mr Alperstein that George hit me on the earhole,' he keeps saying, then storms out.

Granny Tzatzke just sits at a table in the middle of the kitchen and ignores Taffy. Her long grey hair is rolled up in a bun at the back of her head. She has a large double chin, heavily powdered, with a few grey hairs on the smaller of the chins. She sits with her legs wide apart, her dress pulled up above her knees and her stockings held up with garters.

All her recipes are in her head. Her measurements are all with her hand or her fingers. Because of her cooking methods, her chopped herring, matzo ball soup or cold beetroot borsch are a little different each time. My mom once said under her breath, 'These matzo ball are inedible. You could play tennis with them!'

Granny Tzatzke likes pestering our doctor. My mom says Granny Tzatzke is a hypochondriac.

One day I hear my granny calling Dr Ivor Eloff, a young GP who recently came to live in Fort Beaufort, to come to the hotel to check her 'terrible high blood [pressure]'.

Dr Eloff arrives and goes into her room. Melanie, Neil and I stand outside with our ears to the door, listening.

Granny Tzatzke says, 'Ken you please cut my toenails.'

When Dr Eloff leaves, I hear him saying to himself as he walks up the passage to the front of the hotel, 'I'm definitely going into radiology when I've finished this job.'

Granny Tzatzke dies at age eighty-four, having outlived three of her four children.

*

Melanie and I run down to the cottage at morning teatime. We know what Granny Tilly will have for us to eat.

'Garthie and Mellie, I have your favourite butter and Marmite on Marie biscuits for you,' says Granny Tilly. We always have Marie biscuits with butter and Marmite when we visit her at morning teatime.

We call Granny Tilly 'Fivey' because she is exactly five feet tall when she stands up. She can't stand now. She sits in a wheelchair. She is crippled.

My mom says Fivey has multiple sclerosis. She has had it since her late twenties and has been in a wheelchair ever since.

She and my grandpa Philip live in 'the cottage' at the back of the hotel. The cottage has three small rooms. It has very old furniture and very old paintings of landscapes on the walls. To me, everything looks old in the cottage, including them.

*

'Kitty told me that Tilly and Philip married in Potchefstroom in what used to be the Transvaal,' said one of my cousins. 'Tilly said that she worked for her older half-brother in his shop in Uniondale in the Cape. He not only exploited her in his shop, but also wanted to marry her off to one of his friends who was about forty years old, when she was only twenty. Tilly ran away to the Transvaal and met Philip in Potchefstroom. It seems she also had a liaison with another man while in Potchefstroom, but chose Philip. Kitty said that the other man was so furious that he burned down the shed in which they had put their wedding presents. Kitty also said that Philip arrived in South Africa during the Anglo-Boer War at the beginning of the 1900s,' my cousin continued. 'He made his way to the Transvaal and it appears he may have been employed to carry messages on horseback for the Boers as he was too young to fight. Kitty had asked him if he was scared of the fighting. He said no, he was scared of the horse.'

*

When they were young, Tilly and Philip owned a small inn in Bell, near Peddie, where my mother was born. My mother said that Tilly was also the local nurse and counsellor.

'Tilly never had a bad thought in her head,' said my mother. 'She could never do enough for everyone, especially before she developed multiple sclerosis, and couldn't have been a kinder and more gentle person.'

They had three children, my mother being the middle child. Their youngest child, Isadore, whom we called Isky, was a doctor. He was also diagnosed with multiple sclerosis in his late twenties. By the time he was about thirty, he was totally paralysed and bedridden and had huge open bedsores all over his body. He committed suicide when he was thirty-two.

Tilly died of heart failure when she was seventy-two years old. Despite her disability, she had never been demanding, never complained and was always generous to everyone. The worst thing I ever heard her say about anyone was, 'Ven I used to be able to cook, my matzo ball soup vos a lot better then your Grenny Tzatzke's.'

I remember Philip used to help my father in the bar. He was always dressed neatly in a grey three-piece suit with a tie and black shoes that were shiny and polished. He had a serene face, quite wrinkled, and a big nose. He had thick grey wavy hair that was parted in the middle. I don't remember him ever talking – although I'm sure he did – just looking at me benignly. One day, soon after his seventy-fifth birthday, while sitting at the table in the cottage, peeling an apple, Philip dropped the knife and slowly fell off the chair onto the floor, dead.

*

James Moosa enters the courtyard, white cloth over his arm, beating again the rhythm of an African drum.

20

Matzos and Marmite
Malamed's and Rum
Passover was always such fun

We are all sitting around a large table set up in the cottage. My parents, Granny Tzatzke, Granny Fivey in her wheelchair, Grandpa Philip, the Wolffharts and the Gottliebs (the only other Jewish families in town), and Melanie, Neil and I are all singing loudly and merrily, '*Chad, gad, ya*,' over and over again. Those are the only words we know of that song. It is Passover. The part of Passover I really like is all the food – the grated apple with honey, the hard-boiled eggs that you dip in salt water, gefilte fish, chopped herring, chopped liver, brisket, roast lamb, baked potatoes dripping with fat and matzo, which I actually like best with butter and Marmite. Searching for a hidden piece of matzo at the end of the dinner is also fun. We run around the room like wild rabbits turning everything upside down and inside out until one of us finds the hidden matzo wrapped in a cloth serviette.

*

My parents were culturally Jewish rather than religious, but my grandparents took it all more seriously. My mother was a professed atheist and said, 'If there is a God, he is a big shit,' and my father said, 'Who knows and who cares.' However, they did celebrate the main Jewish holidays, the ones that entailed a lot of food. They didn't fast on Yom Kippur, the Day of Atonement. My mother said, 'I can't, I'm diabetic, and if I weren't I'd find some other excuse,' and my father said, 'I have to drink with the customers in the bar.'

*

Grandpa Philip, dressed in a suit, a yarmulke on his head and a decorated white shawl over his shoulders, starts the evening service muttering rapidly from the special Passover book in Hebrew. My dad is dressed in his usual short-sleeved khaki shirt, khaki shorts and brown sandals. The Wolffharts and the Gottliebs are dressed more smartly.

'Daddy, when can we start eating? I'm hungry.'
'Shut up, Garth. Can't you see Grandpa is reading.'

*

Usually the adults, at some point, get bored and tired of waiting, and start to talk and eat and drink, and Philip just carries on speaking very fast in Hebrew. The only part that happens in English is the four questions.

'Vy is dis night different from all udder nights?' asks Philip in his Russian-Yiddish accent, looking directly at us kids.

'Don't know,' we say together.

He reads the answers in Hebrew, while we go back to stuffing our faces. My father is drinking his fifth glass of JB whisky, my mother is slowly sipping her Gordon's gin and tonic in between puffing on her cigarette and the others are all smoking and drinking something.

'Bloemhof is scum,' slurrs my dad to Ronnie Gottlieb.

'No, Max, you're being a bit unfair,' says Ronnie.

'Bloemhof is scum. I say he's scum. He is scum,' he says even louder and slurring even more.

'Max, stop it. The kids,' says my mother.

'I tell you, Bloemhof is scum. He is scum!'

I don't know what they are talking about. Mr Bloemhof has a jewellery shop opposite Paddy Atkinson's chemist. I once bought a watch from Mr

Bloemhof's shop. In the back of the shop, Mrs Bloemhof has a hairdressing setup and my mother sometimes gets her hair done there. Other times she goes to Neville Bezuidenhout, who cuts our hair. We don't get short-back-and-sides haircuts, we get no-back-and-sides and short top. The little hair that is left, Neville smears with Brylcreem.

For the rest of the week, we eat Passover food till we have chopped herring coming out of our ears, but we love it. Although we like matzo with butter and Marmite, we do not like giving up our bread and other forbidden Passover food; we just add to it, except for my mother, who doesn't eat matzo again after the Passover dinner.

'Tastes like cardboard. I'm not eating bloody cardboard!'

21

Home far away
Sadism and cane
Not even time heals the pain

'Next year, when you're nine, you're going to Selbourne College in East London. Isn't that exciting, Toto?' says my mother as we are about to start dinner.

'I don't want to go to boarding school. Why do I have to go to boarding school?'

'Well, you have to have a bar mitzvah when you are thirteen and you will need at least four years to prepare. You don't know any Hebrew. There is no rabbi or synagogue in Fort Beaufort, as you know.'

'You don't even believe in God. Why do I have to have a bar mitzvah? I don't want a bar mitzvah. I don't care if I don't have a bar mitzvah!'

'You have to. You're Jewish. There aren't any Jews who haven't had a bar mitzvah,' says my father firmly.

'I don't care. I don't want one.'

A moment of silence passes.

'Well, when I've had my bar mitzvah, I'm coming straight back to Fort Beaufort.'

I am terrified of going to boarding school. I have heard stories about how new kids are initiated and that boarders are caned more often than the kids who live at home.

'Well, we'll see, Toto,' says my father. 'When you find out what a good school Selbourne is, you won't want to come back. I know. I taught English and Latin at Selbourne. You'll be able to study Latin. You wouldn't be able to study Latin in Fort Beaufort. You don't want to be taught English by an Afrikaner who says one goose, two gooses, do you? That is what you will get at the Fort Beaufort High School. Also you will be able to be with your cousins, the Coopers, and play with David, Peter, Linda and Diane. You'll love it there.'

'I won't!' I leave the dinner table in a huff. I look back and see my parents looking at each other.

*

We arrive at the boarders' residence. My mother helps me unpack my clothes into my grey steel locker. There are seven beds on either side of a row of steel lockers. Each bed has a hard coir mattress, covered with a dark brown blanket. The beds are three feet apart. There are six such rooms in the boarders' residence. The walls of the dorm are painted dark green two-thirds the way up the wall and white to the top. There is a big grassed back yard with trees around the edges. The smell of boiling cabbage is strong.

We go back to the front entrance, where my father is speaking to the principal, Mr Stevens. I kiss my parents and say goodbye to Melanie and Neil. I stand at the entrance of the driveway in my school uniform – grey shorts, a grey shirt and black sandals and a black blazer with white stripes with a badge on the top pocket. I wave as my father drives off. I burst into tears. I run into the dormitory, dive onto my bed and bury my head in the pillow. I don't stop crying for six months.

The first weekend is initiation. It is Saturday morning and still dark. I wake up unable to breathe and can't move. I open my eyes. I am scared. One boy is holding his hand over my mouth, the other holding down my wrists and another my legs.

'Make one sound and we smash your face in. It's polishing time.' They strip off my pyjamas. I lie there naked.

What is polishing? One of the boys gets a tin of black polish and a hard shoe brush and scrapes up a smear of polish. With a leer on his face, he lowers the brush to my genitals and polishes until they are black and sore and then polishes the rest of my body.

'You have to scrub every bit of polish off by breakfast, newpot. If the masters find out about this, you'll be sorry you were born.'

*

All the 'newpots' went through this humiliation and the boarding school masters either never knew or turned a blind eye.

*

'Chips, chips, here comes Stevie,' whispers one of the boys and jumps into his bed.

Chips is the code word for 'A teacher is coming'. It is after lights out.

'Who was talking?' bellows Mr Stevens, the master of the boarding house and school principal.

Silence.

'All right, all of you follow me to my office and don't try to sneak on a pair of underpants under your pyjamas.'

One by one we come out of his office, hardly able to walk straight, hardly able to suppress our tears, after being caned on the buttocks, while the others look on expectantly in fear.

*

The usual method of caning was for one to bend down and to 'offer' the buttocks to be beaten with a three- to four-foot-long straight, rigid cane. The teacher or boarding school master then usually took a step forward and, with a forceful whipping action, directed the cane onto the buttocks. Depending on the 'crime', a maximum of six cuts, as we called them, was permitted. That was followed by a stinging pain, feelings of hate, contempt, violation and trying not to cry. To cry would not have been manly and would have been an admission of weakness and defeat. Usually, caning resulted in painful red raised lines across the buttock, which disappeared after a few days. Occasionally, they drew blood.

That was the beginning of a regular event through my school years. We were caned for too many spelling mistakes, whispering to a classmate during a lesson, talking after lights out, talking in line waiting to go to the dining room for a meal, and countless other reasons.

That was part of life, of growing up, of making 'men' of us, of making us tough, of teaching us who was in command, and teaching us to obey without questioning.

*

One night, I notice that the boy next to me is tapping his blanket from the inside, quite rhythmically and fast.

'What are you doing, James?' I whisper.

'Tossing off, what do you think?'

'What's tossing off?'

'Jerking your terk, milking your lizard, idiot,' he says as he pulls back his blanket to show me.

I know what masturbation is, but have never actually tried it.

'Hey guys, let's all toss off and see who gets the "feeling" first,' he whispers a little louder so everyone can hear.

Then fourteen blankets start tapping. After getting the 'feeling' once then twice then three times, we eventually stop when our penises are too sore to continue and swollen almost to the same width as their length.

The next morning in the shower, one of the older kids says to his friend, 'Gee John, your balls have dropped, your pubes are going curly – you'll be having a wet dream in the next few months.'

*

I realised when I was in medical school that we had described each of the five stages of sexual maturation in precise order of sequence as accurately as a medical textbook.

*

At the end of the first term we are allowed to go home for the Easter holidays. I do not cry that day. My parents come to fetch me. I have packed all my clothes and schoolbooks.

As we are driving along, my mother asks me why I have brought everything home for a week's holiday.

'I'm not going back,' I say softly but firmly, looking down at my little black shoes.

'Come on, Garthie,' my dad says, 'I also didn't want to go back to boarding school when I first started, but then I got used to it, and really liked it, and wouldn't have gone back home even if I had the choice.'

'As soon as I've had my bar mitzvah, I'm coming back home.'

My father says nothing.

*

I wake up earlier than usual. I feel nauseous. I know it is Sunday. The Easter holidays are over and I have to go back to boarding school. I am going to East London by train this time. The train leaves at eleven o'clock in the morning. I get out of bed, get dressed and walk out of the hotel, across the town square, down the path between the museum and the library, towards the swing bridge. I get down to the river. The water is still. There are dragonflies hovering, then suddenly darting off in another direction. I sit under a tree, the tree I would be coming to many times for solace on the day I have to return to boarding school. I still feel nauseous and begin having cramps in my stomach.

Time passes.

'Nicky, where the hell is Toto?' asks my father.

'I think you'll find him at the river,' replies Melanie. 'Near the swing bridge.'

'Which bloody swing bridge?' says my father, becoming more and more agitated.

'The one near the museum.'

My father comes charging down the path. 'Where the bloody hell have you been?'

'Here.'

'What the bloody hell do you think you're doing? You have to get the train at eleven.'

'I know. I don't want to go back to Selbourne. I want to come back home.'

'Well, you can't and you know that. Now get back up to the hotel. Come on, Toto. Once you're there, back with your new friends, it'll be fine. You know that.'

My feelings about the train station are now very different from my earlier memories of going to the station with Beauty. The train is a steam engine. Six hours later, arriving in East London, my hands are black with grime, my hair full of soot and my face looks like I have been playing in the coal shed. Some of the older boys had been smoking and drinking. One boy had vomited in the passage of one of the carriages. I pick up my little brown suitcase, my head bowed, and follow the others to the bus.

22

The fourpenny axe
The battle over land
Falls the Khoikhoi's cuffed hand

During my first year of boarding school, I am in Standard Four and I have to do a history project. I choose to do the War of the Axe, the seventh of the eleven Kaffir Wars, and the one that was fought around Fort Beaufort. I choose the War of the Axe because I know that I can get information and photos from the Fort Beaufort Museum, and I think Lizzie and Ellie Niewenhuys might be able to help me, as they live in the Emgwenyeni flats, from where the axe that started the war was stolen. On the cover of my project book I paint an axe with a brown handle, and a silver blade on a pitch-black background. Thick bright red blood covers half the axe blade and drips onto the background.

*

I am chatting to Lizzie and Ellie on the balcony of their second-storey flat in the Emgwenyeni block opposite the park on Durban Street. Lizzie is a tall, thin woman in her mid-fifties. Her dyed auburn hair, combed back, hangs straight on her shoulders. She wears loose-fitting long dresses with patterns of flowers. Bright red lipstick smears her lips. The people in Fort Beaufort think Lizzie is psychic. They often ask for her advice about matters involving the future and important decisions.

Ellie, her husband, has a big stomach, like my dad's, that hangs over his pants. He is almost bald with only a little hair around the sides and back of his head. He is a nurse at the mental hospital. He always wears a white shirt and black trousers and jacket that are his work clothes. He speaks very slowly and softly in a high-pitched voice with a thick Afrikaans accent. Ellie and Lizzie both call each other 'Giddy'. Maybe it has something to do with the fact that both like their brandy and are often a bit tipsy.

In the flat underneath Ellie and Lizzie is where Mr Holliday's shop was. It was from there that the fourpenny axe was stolen in 1846.

'Garthie,' says Ellie, after taking another drag of the Springbok cigarette held between his thumb and forefinger, 'the War of the Axe was really about land, not about the theft of a silly fourpenny axe. Thousands of Kaffirs were killed. The *soutpiele* were not successful in killing them all with their guns, so they starved them to death by burning their cornfields and their huts. The severe drought of 1846–7 did the rest.'

Mr Holliday's shop now looks like all the other flats in the Emgwenyeni block.

*

Chief Tola sits in his kraal in front of a group of his Xhosa warriors. It is 1846 and tensions have been mounting between him and the British in Fort Beaufort.

'I have spoken to the commander in Fort Beaufort, but they have refused to release my man who stole the axe from Mr Holliday's shop,' says Chief Tola. 'Tsili will be tried in Grahamstown. He must be rescued by whatever means. Leave at once!'

*

Four men, three Xhosas, one of them Tsili, and one Khoikhoi man, handcuffed in pairs, are being led on foot to the gaol in Grahamstown, fifty miles away.

The sun is already scorching the dry earth and it is only around ten o'clock in the morning. The air is still and all is silent except for the heavy breathing and soft rhythmic beat of Chief Tola's men, running.

Spears in hand, they run at a steady pace, but they are anxious. They are now near the black sulphur hot spring seven miles from Fort Beaufort. The smell of sulphur is strong.

One of the men stops, kneels down, puts his right ear to the ground. 'I think they may be near the river now,' he whispers.

As they progress further, soft movement can be heard in the distance. They duck into the bush and run between the mimosa thorn trees and aloes, trying not to be seen. The voices of British soldiers are now clearly audible and growing louder.

The escort party of soldiers and the prisoners takes a rest at the side of the Kat River. Now is the time to attack.

Chief Tola's men spring through the bush. With spears raised, they charge at the soldiers sitting on the ground. Blood spurts in all directions as their spears penetrate the soldiers' chests. With a decisive thrust, the leader's spear stabs the Khoikhoi man, handcuffed to Tsili, in the heart. He immediately drops to the ground dead. He then cuts off the Khoikhoi's hand, allowing Tsili to be set free. Blood drips from the severed hand as it falls through the cuff to the ground.

*

When I was a young child, only a stone on the side of the road bore testimony to this event. The stone was a quarter the size of a headstone, mostly hidden by long grass and bearing no inscription. It was on the road to Grahamstown, seven miles from Fort Beaufort. We often used to pass the spot on the way to swim in the Sulphur Baths, hot springs with pitch-black water that stank of rotten eggs – hydrogen sulphide. Today, the grave has been restored. The inscription on the headstone reads, 'Hottentot Victim of the War 1846', and includes an engraving of a large axe.

There was no obvious evidence that the Emgwenyeni flats had been the site that sparked the start of the War of the Axe. Today, a plaque in front of the building, entitled the Maqoma Trail, documents this history. The Kaffir Wars are now referred to as the Frontier Wars or Wars of Dispossession. A brochure and other plaques around the town now document some of the early history of Fort Beaufort.

23

Tea leaves in cup
Many secrets revealed
Buchu brandy on tap

Lizzie and Ellie spend hours and hours, and many days driving around Fort Beaufort in their little Ford Escort in second gear, going no faster than five miles per hour. They know everything about everybody in Fort Beaufort. Ellie and Lizzie come driving up Campbell Street and slowly pass the hotel.

'Rose doesn't know it yet, but she's going to East London at the end of the month. I'll ask her to get me some of those silky underpants from Woolworths.'

'Giddy, don't you think the town hall needs another coat of paint? I'll speak to Max about it,' says Ellie to Lizzie.

'*Ag* no man, Giddy. I'm sure the council has better things to spend their money on, like a modern *kak* – shit collection system. I'm tired of putting out the bucket for the honey cart every week,' replies Lizzie.

*

I am standing on the veranda of the hotel and wave at them. They both smile and wave back at me. Directly opposite the hotel is the town hall, which looks a bit like an old English castle with a square tower at one end. The paint is looking a little the worse for wear. On three sides of the tower is a large clock with Roman numerals, which strikes the hour with loud dongs; one for each hour, day and night. On hot summer nights when it is hard to sleep, the 'dong' jolts you awake every hour on the hour, usually just when you are finally falling asleep again. Inside the town hall are the mayoral and council chambers and the town cinema – the Kit Kat Cinema – that shows mostly biblical movies and spaghetti westerns.

After the movie, my friends and I spend hours re-enacting the film, particularly the fight scenes. We decide who will be the cowboys and who will be the Indians, then start the 'movie'. My friends never want to play the Indians. I like playing an Indian. They were able to tell how far away the cowboys were by putting an ear to the ground and listening for the sound of the horses' hooves thumping along the desert soil.

The cinema has hard, uncomfortable seats with springs sticking through many of the leather covers. The worst seats are the two rows at the back, which are separated by about twelve feet from the rest: the place reserved for 'non-whites'. There is no slant to the theatre floor, so the seats at the back have the worst view of the screen. 'Black' and 'coloured' people are only allowed to go to Saturday afternoon matinees because there is a curfew for them at ten o'clock at night. If they are found in the town without a good reason, the police will arrest them. The cinema space is also used for many other functions such as the annual police ball, weddings and flower arrangement competitions.

*

'Hey, Giddy, Dulcie Bloemhof is going to win the flower arrangement prize next week,' says Lizzie. 'I saw it in her tea leaves, but didn't tell her. Don't say anything, hey!'

'Is it a year already since the last one in the town hall, Giddy?' asks Ellie, without questioning Lizzie's teacup prediction.

Ellie and Lizzie continue driving slowly down Campbell Street past Dolfie van der Decken's garage.

'Giddy, I was having a drink at the Savoy last week and Gerrit said that Dolfie van der Decken has a crush on Ursula Claasens, Dr Claasens's wife,' squeaks Ellie.

'Man, I already knew that,' she says with a cat-that-licked-the-cream expression.

They pass the Wolffhardts' furniture shop on the left. Ellie looks at Lizzie for some gossip about the Wolffhardts, but there is none. Next to it is Neville Bezuidenhout's barbershop and the office of David Belcher, the town solicitor.

'That David Belcher is useless,' pipes in Ellie. 'Max gave Takhaar Cronje ten beehives to look after for a while because he felt sorry for him. He thought he could make some money from selling honey, after he lost his last job. When Max went to get them, six months later, Takhaar said they were his beehives and wouldn't give them back. Max took Garthie along to learn about the law and see if Belcher could do anything. Belcher just said Takhaar was a bad piece of work and nothing could be done.'

'Why do they call him Takaar, Giddy?' asked Lizzie.

'Because he looks like a bloody porcupine, stupid!'

They drive past Millard's General Store and on cue at ten o'clock Baas Bob walks out of Millard's towards Deane's. Everyone calls Bob Arnold *Baas* Bob. He is a quiet, well-spoken, polite man who wouldn't harm a flea, and not at all a boss type of person. He is about fifty years old, always neatly dressed in a blazer and tie, and lives in a little cottage down Campbell Street with his mother. He is an alcoholic. He works in the hardware section of Millard's General Store. Until the pub opens at ten o'clock, his hands shake uncontrollably. At ten sharp, he has his Richelieu brandy and walks back to the shop, hands steady as a surgeon's.

He does the same at lunchtime and mid-afternoon, and then when Millard's closes at five o'clock, he settles into a comfortable chair in the hotel lounge and drinks himself to sleep. When the pub closes at ten or eleven, I help my father lift him off the chair that he has frequently pissed in, put him in our car and take him home. This happens nearly every night.

'Giddy, just take a slow drive around the town square. I want to see something.'

Ellie puts the car into first gear and turns right in front of Barclay's Bank.

'Just as I thought. There goes Koos van Zyl into Barclays Bank with a bag of money in his hands. He has been embezzling from his boss for months now. Mark my words, the news will come out in thirty-seven days *en dan is die kak in die drinkwater in* – and then the shit is in the drinking water.'

'How do you know he isn't just depositing the business's earnings, man?' asks Ellie.

'Because I know.'

Ellie turns right and drives along the west side of the square past the library and the Fort Beaufort museum, the building that was originally the officers' mess. The museum has many historical photos, documents and clothes from the nineteenth century worn by the townspeople and soldiers, and many weapons used during that time by the British, the Xhosa and the Khoikhoi. There is also a model of a very early Fort Beaufort with streets, the town square and little wooden blocks, which are the buildings such as the officers' mess, the Martello tower and the army barracks. Deane's Hotel isn't on the model. Outside the museum is a large cannon that was supposedly only fired once.

'Hey, Giddy, don't you know any *skinner* – gossip – about Kennedy, the bloke who lives down the road from the Museum?'

'Well, funny you ask right now.' Giddy flicks her bottom false teeth sideways, then quickly back onto her gums. 'That skinny Mr Kennedy who looks like he is always worried that the sky might fall on his head is *pomping* – fucking – the new librarian in the library right next door. I don't know what that pretty young thing sees in him.'

'Jesus, who told you that?'

'Nomhle, who cleans there, was putting the cleaning things back in the cleaning room and there he was, that old man, *broeke om die enkele, steeking* – trousers around his ankles, fucking – her doggie-style. She told me.'

'*Bliksem*, what happened then?'

'Nothing. She put the cleaning things back, closed the door again and went to clean at the co-op shop.'

'What about Ben Nel, Giddy? You know, the one who lives at the bottom of Campbell Street. The one who taught young Garthie to play chess.'

'Of course I know him, man. No.'

'Look Giddy, there's James Clark. I hear he's having a good time with Poppie and *Hoenderhok* – Chickenpen. I saw him sitting in the lounge with them having a drink.' She chuckles and clicks her false teeth back into place.

'Giddy, why do they call her *Hoederhok*?' asks Ellie.

'Because she's tall and skinny, has a small head and walks leaning forward with a back-and-forth movement of her head just like a chicken, man, stupid!'

'I hear all sorts of rumours, you know. The butcher, the baker, the banker and who knows whom else. You probably don't want to know, hey,' says Lizzie.

Ellie smiles.

*

After bowls one Sunday, Lizzie is entertaining the women bowlers in the ladies' lounge, reading their teacups. I stand in the corner and listen. I like to hear Lizzie tell fortunes.

All the bowlers are dressed in their white dresses, brown bowling shoes, round white panama hats with maroon bands and a little badge with the Fort Beaufort crest in the front of the hat. The bowlers meet every Sunday and rotate between the Savoy, the Royal or Deane's. The men gather in the bar and the women in the ladies' lounge.

Lizzie is staring into Betty Jones's teacup, her face sullen. She slides her bottom teeth sideways off the gums, then quickly with her tongue, flicks them back again. She looks up and says, 'I have to tell you what I see. It is not a happy teacup. Very soon, my dear, everyone around you, and including yourself, Betty, will be crying. It will be news of a death.'

There is silence.

'Lizzie had one too many Buchu brandies this morning,' whispers Betty to Sanna.

However, no one else asks to have their teacup read. Some try to start light conversation, but fail. What else can they do but wait for someone to bring sad news?

Within half an hour, a policeman enters the lounge. Everyone knows. He looks puzzled by the silence and stern atmosphere.

'Mrs Jones, I have bad news for you. Your son has just drowned. He dived into the reservoir and never came up. I'm sorry.'

*

I often visit Lizzie at her flat in the Emgwenyeni block. She tells me stories. At every visit, I also ask Lizzie to read my teacup. Lizzie puts a weak cup of Mazawatee tea with lots of milk and sugar in front of me. I can see it has many tea leaves in it. That is good for a reading. I drink my tea as quickly as I can, and hand her the teacup with tea leaf patterns all over the inside. Lizzie stares into the cup. I sit waiting patiently. She chews her teeth, occasionally moving the bottom set sideways, then clicking them back in place. Her flat is dark and has heavy dark oak furniture. It is decorated with Delft and English china plates, jam jars and many things my mom calls bric-a-brac. The flat is always filled with cigarette smoke – Springbok cigarettes – and has the smell of stale cigarette butts. I can smell she has already had her morning tot of Buchu brandy. Lizzie is not talking much today. She starts coughing, and coughs and coughs. She finally stops after coughing up some blood into her handkerchief. She stares at the handkerchief. Lizzie looks sick.

'Auntie Lizzie, are you sick?'

'No, just a smoker's cough, Garthie. But you had better go now.'

A few months later, Lizzie dies from cancer of the oesophagus.

24

Mulberry leaves
Mysteries of childhood
Woven in silk thread

On the dressing table in our bedroom are three shoeboxes. Each box is filled with hundreds of small black silkworm eggs. Through the winter, we inspect them daily to see if the eggs are hatching. They start hatching in spring, but we don't know when spring starts, so we just check them every day. The days are getting longer and the sun is rising earlier. That we do know.

'They've started to hatch,' I hear, as Melanie shakes me awake early one morning.

Neil and I jump out of bed and the three of us stand staring into the shoebox. Tiny black worms are crawling around slowly.

'We'd better get some mulberry leaves at Brian and Marjory's house,' I say.

They are school friends who have a huge mulberry tree in their garden. Many kids in the town keep silkworms. There are quite a few mulberry trees around to feed the silkworms, but most of us get our leaves from Marjory and Brian's tree. They have the largest tree in the town, which also has the biggest and sweetest mulberries. When we aren't picking leaves for our silkworms, we are eating mulberries. Often, much to our parents' dismay, we return home with our clothes, hands and faces stained purple.

We are quite good at caring for our silkworms. When the eggs hatch, we carefully pick up the tiny black worms with a fine paintbrush and put them, one by one, onto a fresh leaf. There are usually hundreds of silkworms. As they grow and change colour, we separate them into pure white ones and white ones with black stripes. We let most of the silkworms spin a cocoon, but some we put onto a flat piece of cardboard, usually cut into the shape of a heart. The silkworm tries to spin a cocoon, but as there are no sides to anchor the silk onto, the silk ends up covering the piece of cardboard. This comes as the shape of a heart, or close to. We also make the silkworms spin on a square, or a circle. We spin the silk off the cocoon by putting the cocoon into warm water, getting the end of the thread and winding it onto a cotton reel or piece of wood. That kills the pupa inside.

We also know that to have silkworms for the next season, we have to leave some of the cocoons so that the pupas can change into moths, which eat their way out of the cocoon and then mate with other moths.

The female lays hundreds of eggs, which we keep to start the whole cycle over again. Sometimes our curiosity and mischievousness get the better of us, and when the moths are mating with their rear ends joined together, we pull them apart and watch the creamy-pink coloured semen spray all over the box.

When we are too lazy to spin the silk ourselves, we take them to the Sinclairs' house and return a few days later to be presented with a beautiful thick skein of yellow silk. We put the silk on our cupboard and then usually forget about it. Many kids in the town take their cocoons to the Sinclair sisters to spin the silk off the cocoons.

The Sinclairs live at the southern end of town in a little cottage on Campbell Street that has a shady veranda in the front. Two windows face the street and the curtains are always drawn. Whenever we take cocoons to them to spin, it is always old Mrs Sinclair who takes the cocoons and returns the silk. She is about eighty years old, small and bent over, and wears her grey hair in a little bun at the back. She wears cashmere cardigans and dull tartan skirts. She always has a sweet smile for us, and speaks with a poncy English accent.

*

When I was young, about a third of Fort Beaufort's residents were of English-speaking descent and were more English than the English, with habits such as playing tennis on Sunday afternoons, accompanied by tea and scones.

Two-thirds of the town's residents were Afrikaners. In general, Afrikaners considered themselves to be the pioneers of the country and sometimes used to use the Bible to justify apartheid.

The differences were also well displayed on voting days. The Nationalist party voting booth was manned by Afrikaans-speaking 'whites' and the opposition United Party booth by English-speaking 'whites'. The people in the queues picking up 'how to vote' pamphlets mirrored those manning the voting booths. As a result, my father said, the member for Fort Beaufort was always the Nationalist party candidate. At that time, only 'whites' were allowed to vote.

*

'Hello, Mrs Sinclair, we've brought you more cocoons to spin for us. Mom said to tell us how much it is,' says Melanie.

'Thank you, Melanie. How sweet of you. Tell your mother, dear, that I will collect the payment from her next time I see her – possibly at bowls on Sunday afternoon, during afternoon tea,' says Mrs Sinclair.

*

We never saw the Sinclair sisters. We didn't know anyone who ever saw the Sinclair sisters. That was my recollection. I also never asked anyone about them and obviously chose to live with this perception. I had read the story of Rapunzel trapped in the witch's tower and wondered...?

25

> What shall become
> of brutes and bastards
> The child's curse!

Melanie and I are sitting in the hotel courtyard drinking Hubbly Bubbly on a cool autumn day. It is school holidays, just after my tenth birthday.

'Roger Crane is dead, Roger is dead, Roger is dead,' Neil runs towards us chanting. 'I've got good news. Roger is dead!'

Neil, Melanie and I jump around, rejoicing. Roger Crane died in a car accident at the age of thirty-seven.

*

Roger Crane was a foreman at the Fort Beaufort Divisional Council. He lived at home with his parents all his life. He was a tall strong man who had thick brown hair parted in the middle, a full moustache covering his upper lip and a handsome face in a rough kind of way. A typical beer drinker's pot belly hung over his short khaki pants.

Roger had been captain of the Fort Beaufort rugby team and played prop. All the small towns in the area had their own rugby team and throughout the winter played matches against each other. There was a ritual to those rugby matches. Both teams met at one of the town's pubs at least an hour before the game. They got to know each other over four or five beers. Then they went to the rugby field, played their match, often with much bloodletting, and left the field arm in arm.

The after-match drinking would continue until the early hours of the morning. There was much debauchery, singing of dirty songs, fist fights, vomiting, finally ending in a drunken stupor, asleep on the stairs, the chairs, the floor or wherever there was a vacant spot. There was no better way to spend a Saturday.

*

Four years earlier on a Sunday around lunchtime. The dry summer heat beats down while the flies buzz around, looking for any drop of moisture they can find. I am playing in the shaded courtyard next to the bar with Melanie and Neil.

Roger Crane is sitting on a bar stool in the bar, drinking a Lion lager. 'There's no way I'll drink next to a Kaffir in the bar! Kaffirs stink!' I hear him bellow with slightly slurred speech.

*

That was Roger's reaction to South Africa's republic debate.

At one point, after my father had hired and fired the fifth 'white' barman in seven months, he decided that it was time to employ a 'coloured' or Xhosa barman – probably through desperation, maybe economically driven, or even possibly partially making a political statement. The loyal patrons were outraged.

Roger Crane, as always, was very vocal. 'No way is a Kaffir going to serve me a drink in the bar!' However, he didn't seem to mind Geography, the new Xhosa waiter, serving him a drink if he was sitting in the lounge, or a 'black' waitress serving him dinner in our dining room.

All my friends' parents had 'black' servants who cleaned their houses, made their beds, cooked all their meals and looked after them and their children. My brother, my sister and I each had our own 'black' nanny.

In Fort Beaufort, 'black' people did all the work. 'White' people had better clothes, they had cars, they told 'black' people what to do, and the 'black' people always said, '*Ja, baas*' or 'Yes, master', and my father called them savages. We were taught in school that there would always be poor people. The Bible said so.

'Joshua 9:23 – the "blacks" will be the "hewers of wood and drawers of water for the house of my God",' said one of our teachers. We were taught that what the Bible meant was that 'black' people were inferior to 'whites' and would always remain so.

*

James Moosa beats the gong in the usual manner to signal lunch. Roger staggers out of the bar into the courtyard, his back to the dining room. His stomach hangs over his short khaki pants. He stands swaying with his fists clenched, his eyes piercing, blood on his knuckles.

Geography is standing opposite him, blood dripping from his mouth, his fists clenched, but not moving, shouting, 'You can't do thet. I'm not en enimal!'

Roger punches him in the face again. Geography dares not hit back. He knows he will be taken to the police station and beaten. If he is lucky, he will live and spend a few months in gaol. Geography, blood dripping from his face, walks away, head bowed. My father does nothing. I stand there, fists clenched, but not able to move. I feel sick. I wish Roger Crane dead. I am six years old.

Max and Rose Alperstein's wedding.

Max Alperstein (left) in the Second World War.

Rose Alperstein.

Fort Beaufort Council in front of Town Hall. Max seated, middle, front row.

My maternal grandparents Tully and Philip.

Beauty Baardman.

Beauty Baardman outside her hut near Fort Beaufort.

Melanie and Neil Alperstein.

The author, about eighteen months old, in front of coal shed.

Primary school class photo, 1958, author in the middle in front of and to the right of teacher.

The author, about eight years old, in front of hotel.

Remembrance Day at the War Memorial, mid-1950s.

Max Alperstein as mayor on a carnival float.

The author (middle) as a teenager.

26

Trading wares and fares
From far they bring
Lonely lives murky tales

There were few good reasons to stay in or visit Fort Beaufort, and so the majority of people who sought accommodation in the hotel were *smouse* – travelling salesmen – selling their wares to the local townspeople.

The salesmen came from the big cities like Cape Town and set up their wares on long trestle tables in the sample room at the back of the hotel. People would view their goods and place an order for a watch, or a china bowl, or some trinket for which they had waited a year.

Louis Levy, the salesman, assured them they would get their goods in less than three months. The people of Fort Beaufort were in no hurry.

*

'Hey, Lena, you should go and see all the stuff Louis Levy has in the sample room, man. *Gaan jy iets koop* – Are you going to buy something?'

'*Nee man. Ek kan nie. Ek is 'n kleurling* – No, man. I can't. I'm a "coloured".'

I look at Lena, not quite sure what the connection is. She looks sad and walks back to the pantry.

Louis Levy is sitting in the courtyard, drinking a Johnny Walker on the rocks. 'Rose, can you have a ham and cheese sandwich sent up to my room. You know, my ulcer – small meals frequently. I have to call Beryl and the kids in Cape Town. I call them every night at seven.'

'Yes, of course, Louis.'

Under her breath I hear the Queen say, 'My arse he's got an ulcer. My arse he has to eat small frequent meals. Never seen him eat a small meal yet. And *nogal* – moreover, he's just a pig!'

I look at Louis Levy. He does have a fat stomach.

*

I have just got back from watching a rugby match between Fort Beaufort and Somerset East. Fort Beaufort won. I hate watching or playing rugby, but my dad took me to see the match. He is president of the Fort Beaufort Rugby Club. At boarding school, I play rugby. Everyone has to. Only kids with disabilities or other diseases can play soccer. I play hooker. I am always the last into the scrum, the last to leave and try my best to avoid getting the ball.

I walk into the courtyard and hear Henry Nel. 'Jerusalem, Jerusalem,' he is singing at the top of his voice.

I peep into the lounge just off the courtyard. Henry is sitting alone and looking up at the ceiling as he sings. Henry is another travelling salesman. When he isn't showing his wares in the sample room, he sits in the lounge directly off the courtyard and sings his favourite song – 'Jerusalem'. I don't know if he knows any other songs. Sometimes some of the other customers in the hotel come and watch him, but most of the time he is all by himself.

I am standing in the doorway of the lounge. At the end of a verse, I clap loudly. Henry doesn't seem to hear. He carries on, oblivious.

*

Herr Holtz, also a travelling salesman, sits by himself in the dining room. It is dinnertime. He is known for his straight talk and swearing. Everyone in the dining room at the hotel is on tenterhooks as Herr Holtz takes his first bite of food. They are probably secretly hoping he will disapprove. This evening they are not disappointed.

'*Das ist Scheiße* – That is shit! Tek it bek!' he bellows.

Katie, the waitress, has anticipated the outburst and, with a straight face, picks up his plate and walks back to the kitchen through the swing doors.

Herr Holtz introduces himself as Herr Holtz. He writes his name in the accommodation book – Herr Holtz. Nobody knows him by any other name. He is a short and thin man who walks very straight up, leaning slightly backwards. He has black hair, parted down the middle, and a little Hitler-type moustache, and speaks with a thick German accent. He grew up in Germany and fought for the Germans in the First World War and the Allies in the Second World War. He is still drawing a pension from both. On top of all that, Herr Holtz is also Jewish.

*

It is a balmy midsummer evening. Goosens appears in the courtyard. He is a tall man who stoops forward slightly when he walks. He has straight greying brown hair that is combed back and plastered down with Brylcreem. He always wears a white shirt and tie, a brown corduroy jacket, long khaki pants and *veldskoene* – suede leather boots. He joins Melanie, Neil and *Oom* Hendrik at the table.

'*Bring my 'n nommer 17*,' he orders in Afrikaans. Lion lager is also referred to as number 17. If one inverts the word Lion, the 'I' and the 'L' look like 17.

'Hello, *Oom* Goosen. Are you back in town to do some selling in the sample room again?' inquires my brother.

'Yes, man, Neil. I've just got back from South West.'

'Where in South West – Windhoek, Walvis Bay, Swakopmund?'

'Everywhere, man. You should have seen the size of the mosquitoes in the Okavango swamps.'

Neil, Melanie and I are sitting with Goosens, drawing out more and more fantastical stories from him.

'They were as big as butterflies, Garth. I know you don't believe me, but damn, there's another one on me.' He pretends to hit something the size of a bird on his shoulder.

Goosens, like Holtz, only uses his surname. His stories get bigger and better with every Lion lager he drinks.

'Let me tell you something,' Goosens says in a very confiding manner. 'On nights like this I go into the shower, grab my stick and whack away until I shoot shit and snot all over the place.'

We smile sheepishly.

*

It is a hot, dry summer's day in 1880. Two men are sitting in the bar of the Beaufort Cottage Hotel on the Koonap River near Fort Beaufort.

'What was your name again, sir?' inquires Corporal Jones. Jones, an imposing man, dressed in his red and black soldier's uniform, holds a glass of red wine in his left hand.

'Louis Goldman, sir,' replies the man. 'I em on my vay to Fot Beaufot to sell my vares. I heff knives, spoons and forks, plates of all sizes ent shapes ent even some very fine jewellery. How much ferder is it to Fot Beaufot, sir?'

The Beaufort Cottage is a small hotel, but has provided many a traveller with comfortable accommodation. Fresh fish and eels from the river provide fine food for the residents and some of the farmers who come by for a drink.

'Not too far, Goldman. You said you were from Cape Town.' He is starting to slur now, after a glass too many. 'You would then have heard of the death of that Kaffir Chief Maqoma on Robben Island a few years ago? He was the ugliest Kaffir you ever did see, and a cattle thief and a fucking drunkard to boot, but probably the best Kaffir warrior in the British Kaffreria. He didn't get involved in the War of the Axe in 1846, but not even Sir Harry Smith, ruthless scoundrel as he was, could budge him out of the Waterkloof. Sir Harry had to leave the colony and return to England with his tail between his legs!' He lets out a loud guffaw. 'Maqoma had a new war strategy. He ambushed our men, fucking shot them before they knew anyone was around, then stabbed the rest with assegais. He would not come out into the open. Just

ambush! Fucking ambush, ambush, ambush! That's how he did it, sire. We did not know how the fuck to cope with that. Mr – what is your name again? You're not from these parts, are you? From whence do you come?' he asks with an even more pronounced slur.

'Cep Town.'

'No, Mr. What is your name again?, I can hear your accent's not from this country nor from mine.'

'Goldman, sir. I em from Vilna in Lithuania, sir.'

'Where the fuck is that, Goldman?'

27

> The kudu's leg hangs
> Muscles dissected
> Stories revealed concealed

Oom Hendrik is teaching me how to make biltong – dried cured meat (jerky).

'Garthie, the best piece of biltong is from the *rugstring*, the long muscle down the middle of the back. Here we have the leg of a kudu, but that will do.'

George McCarthy had shot a kudu and given my father one of the legs with which to make biltong. *Oom* Hendrik has tied it up, hanging upside down, from one of the beams in the courtyard.

'*Oom* Hendrik, can I cut the biltong this time?' I ask eagerly.

'*Ja*, but remember you must cut the muscles out along the cracks between them, so you get a nice *stuk* – piece.'

*

I had no idea at that time that I would be studying medicine and in our second year dissect a human body. When it came to the leg, I recognised all the muscles and their shapes and attachments to bone from all the dissections I had done on kudus' and cows' legs.

*

While I am dissecting the muscles from each other and off the thigh bone and neatly putting these in a large white enamel dish, my brother and sister arrive. They settle into chairs nearby, order a Fanta orange from Geography, and watch. It is five o'clock and the regulars are starting to arrive to begin their evening of drinking. It is midwinter and the sun is starting to set.

Biltong must be made in the winter since, after curing the meat, it has to be hung in a dry, cool place to continue the curing and hardening process. In Fort Beaufort's summers of 110 to 120F, the meat would rot.

'Now, Garthie, you need to wipe all the blood from the muscles, man.' Hendrik picks up a muscle at one end with his left hand. With the other hand he makes a ring with his thumb and middle finger and gently and slowly runs the ring down the muscle to squeeze off the blood. 'Nice,' he remarks after he has prepared each piece and gently laid it down into a second white enamel basin.

When a layer covers the bottom, he sprinkles it with a lot of salt and pepper. Sometimes he also uses coriander seeds. This he repeats with each layer.

'Now, Garthie, we need vinegar and brown sugar, man. Never use white sugar. Must be brown, man.' He dissolves a cup of brown sugar in a large bottle of vinegar and pours it over the basin of meat. 'Nice,' he repeats, and pats the meat. 'We leave it now for two days in the pantry where it's nice and cool, man.'

There is a small balcony off one of our bedrooms upstairs. My father has enclosed a section of it with fine gauze and fitted it with a gauze door. That is our biltong-curing cage. Across the top are wires in straight lines, each with multiple S-shaped hooks made from fencing wire. The thick end of the meat is hung on the wire hook. The gauze keeps the flies out. Depending on the temperature, total curing and drying usually takes two to three weeks. However, we kids cannot wait that long and also we like it pretty raw. As soon as a firm skin forms on the outside, which happens in two to three days, we remove it from the cage and bite into it with our molars, tearing off pieces of partially cured kudu. This makes our mother angry.

'You bloody kids are bloody cannibals,' she says, taking another draw of her cigarette. She can't stand the sight of blood in meat. She always orders her meat well done. 'You know what I mean: cremated,' she always says to the waiter.

*

We have dinner late that night. Usually we kids eat dinner in the dining room before the hotel guests. It is about eight-fifteen and in walks Hendrik Swart.

'I've got a story to tell you, man,' he says with great excitement in his thick Afrikaner accent. He walks behind our table, which is against the back wall of the dining room, then bends down and sniffs. He moves ten inches along the wall at the juncture with the floor and sniffs again.

We watch with great interest.

'I can smell burning. No, not here. Here, maybe? No, not here.' He moves another ten inches along the wall with his backside in the air and sniffs again. 'No, not here. Man, I could smell something burning, but I couldn't quite tell where it was coming from, man. So I went around the whole hall, sniffing bit by bit. I was sure I'd find where the burning was coming from, man.' Hendrik proceeds to sniff along the crack between the wall and the floor of the entire dining room, ten inches at a time.

We watch on in silence, waiting for something to happen. After a while we start to giggle, but he continues unperturbed, searching all around the dining room until he reaches his starting point, half an hour later.

'I've found it, man,' he blurts out excitedly on his last double sniff.

We all clap and cheer and can't stop our giggling.

'What did you find?' Melanie manages to insert between giggles.

'I located the fire, man. They brought out buckets of water and one chap had a little red fire extinguisher at his house, and we put out that fire, man!' he says, looking very proud of himself.

Hendrik is a skinny man, at least six foot tall, who has a darkly tanned face and arms. He has a thin pencil-line black-grey moustache and often a just-having-sucked-on-a-lemon expression. Every day he wears long khaki pants, a long-sleeved khaki shirt with the sleeves rolled up, a big khaki suede hat tipped forward on his head and *veldskoene*. We do not know much about Hendrik, or we haven't been told much about Hendrik. He has been staying at the hotel for the past three months.

'He's still a bachelor and fifty – too young for you,' I hear my mother telling ninety-year-old Miss Rowley.

*

One morning, just after breakfast, Melanie, Neil and I are sitting in the courtyard. *Oom* Hendrik arrives.

'*Oom* Hendrik, what do you do, man?' I ask.

'Man, Garthie, I was a prospector for semi-precious stones in South West Africa, man.'

'What's a prospector, *Oom* Hendrik?'

I shouldn't have asked. Hendrik disappears to his room on the second floor of the hotel.

He reappears twenty minutes later with a little brown bag. 'Come with me, kids, man.'

We follow him to the back of the hotel. He suddenly stops and puts out his right arm, motioning us to stop. He bends down, opens his bag and brings out a hammer-like implement with sharp points on both sides. He grabs a stone from the ground, holds it up, turns it round and round with that sour look on his face. He taps the stone with this hammer next to his right ear. He puts it down. 'No, not this one.' He repeats this a number of times, until he finally says, 'I think, maybe, this one.'

He puts the stone onto a large rock nearby and hits the stone firmly. It cracks open and looks the same inside as it looked outside.

'Damn, man, not this one. In the South West desert, I found so many agates and tiger's eyes and all sorts of very pretty-coloured semi-precious stones, man. And that's how you find them.'

'You must be very rich, *Oom* Hendrik. And did you find any diamonds?' I ask.

'Yes, man, so many diamonds in South West, Garthie.'

We three look at each other, wondering whether to believe *Oom* Hendrik.

We get back to the hotel to find Babs sitting in the courtyard, having a gin and tonic with my mother.

'Mind if I join you young ladies, man?' says Hendrik, pulling up another cane chair. He clicks his fingers in the air, looking straight ahead, and calls out 'Waiter!'

Geography hears him from near the bar and walks briskly to where they are sitting.

'A Johnny Walker on the rocks, waiter,' he orders, still without looking at the waiter.

'*Ja, baas*,' says Geography. He walks briskly back to the bar and returns with a whisky on the rocks.

'I've got a riddle for you kids,' said Babs, rolling her 'r' with her strong Afrikaner accent. Babs is a short, stout woman in her mid-fifties with a square head and short, wavy brown-dyed hair. Her real name is Betty Brevis, but everyone just calls her Babs.

'What, Tannie Babs?' asks Melanie.

'What's a *drol dreper dreskas*?'

'Dunno,' we always reply.

'*Drie drolle op 'n dreskas* – three pieces of shit on a dressing table,' she replies, followed by loud guffaws.

We reply with coy giggles.

A week later, the whole scenario is repeated again.

Hendrik and Babs get married.

'Each thought the other had money, but neither did,' says my mother to Audrey Delponte, and gives a somewhat sardonic cackle.

'So what happened with them then, Rose?'

'I don't know, but it must have been a rude shock for them both to find out.' Another cackle followed by a sputum-bubbling smoker's cough.

28

Passing time
Beer and cheap wine
Blood knuckles

'*Gee my bier. Van die rak af* – Give me a beer. From the shelf,' Whitey orders me in a gruff voice and slams his fist on the bar counter.

From the time I turn twelve, my father puts me to work more regularly behind the bar counter during school holidays. I listen to the drunks telling the same stories over and over again and never get bored. During quiet periods, I practise playing darts and snooker.

'Whitey, did you hear that Koos van der Merwe who lived at 13 Campbell Street went to hell when he died?' asks George Ferreira with a straight face.

'*Nee*,' replies Whitey.

'Well, old Koos asked the devil if he could have a few days' special leave to go back to Fort Beaufort to fetch his blankets.' George cracks up laughing at his own joke. He feels he had told it very well, and in fact he thinks he has Whitey for a while.

'*Dis net 'n grap, nê*, George – That's just a joke, isn't it, George?' inquires Whitey with a somewhat sheepish, puzzled look on his face.

Whitey only drinks his beer warm, no matter what the temperature is. It is not clear why he is called Whitey. He is a very tall, skinny and darkly tanned Afrikaner who wears the same clothes, no matter the weather; a brown felt hat, long-sleeved khaki shirt, long khaki pants and *veldskoene*. He walks in long strides with a dip at the end of each stride.

He sits on a bar stool and looks up at Harry Els. '*Wat sê jy, jou ou stuk biltong* – What do you say, you old piece of biltong?'

'Whaadoya mean a piece of auld dried meat? Aahm nod a piece of biltong!' drawls Harry with seriously slurred speech.

This draws a round of laughter from all the other soaks in the pub. Furthermore, it really annoys Harry, which makes his slurred speech and unsteady gait worse, making the crowd laugh louder. It usually ends up with Harry emptying his beer glass into someone's face and a fist fight. Harry has dark brown hair, a thick moustache, and always has a few days' stubble. He has a walk that could compete with Whitey's. His friends call it 'the ten-to-two' walk.

*

During my medical studies, I learnt that the effects of excessive alcohol on the cerebellum of the brain resulted in slurred speech and an unsteady gait on a broad base. Harry was probably as ignorant as I was then that his problems were due to alcohol.

*

Bun Wilson downs his 'number 17'. 'Who wants a game of darts?' His smile exposes his toothless mouth.

Gert Potgieter always likes a challenge, especially when he knows he can win. 'I'll take you on, Bun, but first I must do my stretches.' He stands up straight, lifts his arms above his head and then hinges at the hips, his belly now hanging like a full-term pregnancy. Somehow he manages to put both his hands flat on the floor. He is very proud of this bar trick. 'I bet none of you can do that,' he boasts.

There is a general and muffled 'No, no, no,' response from the rest of the customers.

'OK, Bun, you go first. What are you going for?'

'Double four, double four, double four.' Bun only tries to throw double fours and therefore usually loses.

*

I am doing a shift in the bar helping Hilary Thomson, the barman, who is himself an alcoholic. Hilary is a short man with short black hair, a neat black moustache, always neatly dressed in a blazer, white shirt and tie. My dad is sitting, chatting to the customers. It is the shift change-over and Mr Shultz is taking over from Hilary. Mr Shultz arrives a little late. He is short and fat, wears thick glasses and is about sixty years old.

I hear a noise coming from the bar toilet. I go to investigate. I enter the toilet, which stinks of old piss. It always does. I see Hilary slamming his fist into Mr Shultz's nose, which is already bleeding. There is blood everywhere and Mr Shultz is trying to put his hands in front of his face. I run out and shout to my dad to come quickly. My father comes in. I stand at the door and watch. They are wrestling. My father lifts his arms and karate chops Hilary Thomson's hand and now it spews blood as well. I start to feel sick and think I am going to vomit. Old Mr Shultz is Joy Begbee's step-dad. What am I going to say to her?

*

A number of years later in my fourth year of training at medical school, we visited Slater House, a residential facility for alcoholics. The first person I saw when I walked in was Hilary Thompson, still with his neat moustache, blazer and tie. It was an awkward moment.

29

A legacy not desired
Neither just nor fair
Leaves a trail mired

Sakkie throws a glass of cold water into Mickie's face. Mickie is perched on a barstool in the 'coloured' bar of the hotel and is in a drunken stupor. The entrance to the bar for 'coloured' people is around the corner from the bar where 'whites' drink, and is situated down a narrow lane. There is a sign on the corner with an arrow and the word *Kleurlinge* – Coloureds. (Xhosa people are not allowed to drink in the town.)

The bar is dark and dingy, very sparse, and has peeling paint falling from the walls. There is no furniture except for a few old reject bar stools with torn plastic seats, and there is an odour of cheap, stale wine mixed with the smell of old tobacco ash. I stand next to Michael, the 'coloured' barman, and watch. I spend many hours in the 'coloured' bar during my school holidays, helping serve the customers and observing the goings-on.

'*Jou ma se moer* – Your mother's cunt,' Mickie manages to utter, barely able to raise his upper eyelids, but slightly exposing his bloodshot eyes. His head flops forward again and he drifts back into semi-consciousness.

Sakkie lets out a peal of laughter and orders a glass of Old Brown sherry, locally referred to as OB. Sakkie has no front teeth. He wears a soft tartan peak cap and frequently smells of OB.

Mickie, who suffers from schizophrenia, spends most of his day wandering around, telling himself jokes and stories, and then laughing out aloud to himself. Every time he laughs or chuckles, the few teeth left in his mouth shake and rattle and come close to falling out of their sockets. Nobody, including himself, knows how old he is. He has a sparse grey beard and sparse curly grey hair usually hidden by a grey peaked cap. Come winter or summer, he wears the same old jacket, old suit pants and shoes with the soles flapping up and down as he walks.

Mickie is a keen fisherman and even wears his jacket when he goes fishing. All the fish he catches he puts in his jacket pockets. On a good day, he fills up all his pockets and walks around Newtown, showing off all his fish to friends in the township. There are times when he shows off for days, keeping them in his pockets all that time, steadfastly refusing to wash the jacket. After tolerating the smell for some time, his friends throw away the fish and remove his clothes while he sleeps, and wash them for him.

Tollie, the local cobbler, staggers into the 'coloured' bar. Tollie is going bald and has a little scarf around his neck. He also manages to maintain a two-day stubble on his face.

He saunters up to his best mate, Sakkie, and orders Michael, *'Gee hom nog 'n OB, en een vir my, kontkop* – Give him another OB, and one for me, cunt-head.'

Tollie and Sakkie, arms around each other's shoulders, sip their OB.

I notice Sakkie has a recent scar on the left side of his neck from behind the ear, round the front of the neck to the hollow at the top of his breastbone. 'Sakkie, what happened to you?' I ask.

'Tollie and I had a fight and Tollie tried to kill me,' he says and lets out another reel of laughter.

'Yes,' Tollie chips in, 'I tried to kill him!' joining Sakkie in a hearty cackle.

They toast each other, drain their glasses and leave the bar arm in arm.

Mickie, Sakkie and Tollie live in Newtown. Newtown has a rugby field of sorts with very little grass and many potholes. Newtown has a 'coloured' rugby team that plays against 'coloured' teams from surrounding towns. Mickie loves watching and supporting and cheering his team. He also doesn't like his team to lose. If he sees that the opposition team is about to score, he runs onto the field and either intercepts the ball or grabs it from the player and runs off with the ball into the bush, both teams in hot pursuit.

*

On a fine autumn day in 1939 Katie and Tollie are sitting in front of her little shelter in Blinkwater, a small village in the Kat River Valley.

'Don't be so sad, Tollie. You are probably better away from that verneeker – cheat – Fenner-Solomon,' says Katie.

'He took my sitplekkie I had in Seymour, just like he has from so many Hotnots for so many years. I went to borrow money from him to pay for my cow I bought at the auction. He was even the auctioneer. He said I must pay him back in three weeks. He says, "Sign here." I just make a cross because I can't write. How the hell must I get the money in three weeks?'

'What a shit. What happened then, Tollie?'

'Three weeks comes and I have only three pounds. He says, "You signed here on this piece of paper. Your land and house are security for the loan. If you don't pay me back in full in three weeks, you'll hand over your land and house to me." I say, "I didn't sign no such kak – shit." He says, "Yes you did and you have two weeks to move out. I've already sold the property to James Smith. He'll be moving in Monday two weeks. Now get out of my office. I'm busy. Go!" he says.'

'That land in the Kat River Valley was given to us Hotnots van die Kaap – but that's over now! Now almost all of it has been stolen from us and given to die wit mense – the white people. He even steals from the Boere – Afrikaners! What kind of a lawyer is that?'

'Well, Tollie, you're here now. Hey, who the vok – fuck – gave you the name Tollie?'

'I worked for some Boere on their farm when I was a jongetjie – young child. They called me Tollie.'

'Now there's no work here in Blinkwater, but there is in eBofolo. You must learn to make shoes and you'll make a lot of money from the white people. But don't take their liquor as payment. No perske brandewyn – peach brandy – only money.'

On the east side of the town square on Campbell Street is a small, empty building across a stream of raw sewage that comes from a small group of houses at the back of the shops on Campbell Street.

'That would be a good shop for a cobbler, Sakkie,' says Tollie to his friend Sakkie, who had learnt the trade in Graaf-Reinet where he grew up.

'Ja, man, I could teach you, easy. Let's ask Baas Gerrit,' replies Sakkie.

They cautiously walk around the corner into Baas Gerrit's shop. Baas Gerrit is sitting in his office near the shop counter. He looks up and sees them outside his door. Gingerly, they knock.

'Ja, Hotnot?'

'Baas Gerrit, ag please, Baas Gerrit, can Sakkie and I please use the old house at the back of your shop to set up a shoe shop – fix shoes, not sell them of course, samblief – please, Baas Gerrit?' pleads Tollie.

'What's a Hotnot like you know about fixing shoes? The Boere were right: you lot are a bunch of vermin who should have been exterminated,' he says. 'No concept of land ownership, Christianity, loyalty, nothing,' he continues under his breath. 'Ja, OK, you can. Nou vok weg – Now fuck off!' he says impatiently.

'Thank you baas, dankie baas,' Tollie says, backing off slowly with his head bowed and his hands in front of him in the praying position.

30

The blind mole
Sees not
A double-barrelled hole

Sergeant Pieter Wessels falls asleep in the chair in the garden. The double-barrelled shotgun starts to slip out of his hands. It is about seven o'clock in the evening, the sun is just above the horizon and the temperature has cooled down to about 105F. Sergeant Wessels is seventy-two years old and still employed by the Security Police Special Branch. He is a slim, tall man with short grey hair and a grey Hitler-style moustache. He goes to work every day in Alice, which is fourteen miles from Fort Beaufort and is the town where Fort Hare University is located. After his morning cup of coffee and a Springbok cigarette, he puts his head on his desk and falls asleep. The staff at the office then wake him up for lunch and afternoon tea, and at five o'clock to go home.

Every day, except on the few occasions a year when it rains, on getting home, Pieter loads his gun, takes a chair outside and places it in front of a mole-hole mound. With the shotgun in one hand and a glass of Buchu brandy in the other, he sits and waits for the mole to rear its head. When it does, he pulls both triggers and blows it to pieces. This happens very rarely, since moles do most of their burrowing at night.

Pieter is married to Marie, a nursing sister with one of the kindest hearts, but foulest mouths, in the town. Marie is tall, slim and always smiling. When a new doctor comes to town, which happens regularly, the nurses time Marie with a stopwatch to measure how long it will take for her to thoroughly disgust or embarrass the unsuspecting doctor.

*

Koos Wessels, Pieter and Marie's son and my friend, went to Rhodes University in Grahamstown to do a Bachelor of Arts – aka Bugger All. Koos, who had been a very gentle boy and polite to all adults at all times, soon got into the university spirit. He told me how at the local movie house he would smuggle in cans of beer, get drunk and, while watching old Second World War movies, would cheer the Germans, and shout obscenities and throw beer cans at the screen when the British appeared. He was frequently booted out of the movie house. This was all done with tongue in cheek. Grahamstown was renowned for being a particularly English South African town.

Koos also learned how he could use a tickey coin (threepence), with a hole drilled through and string attached, to make phone calls from a public telephone box. He called everywhere, including myself in Cape Town and friends overseas with the use of that one tickey on a string.

The police got wind of this practice and one day caught him with tickey-coin-on-string in hand.

'Your name, boy,' said the policeman, looking very sternly at Koos.

'Koos Wessels, sergeant,' he replied very politely.

After obtaining the usual details, the sergeant asked, 'And who is your father?'

'Sergeant Pieter Wessels, Special Branch, South African Police Force, sir.'

The policeman, looking aghast, was left speechless for a short while. 'You had better not let me catch you doing this again, *hoor* – hear me!'

31

> Muddy waters at first light
> The unsuspecting eel
> The hook does bite

'Toto, Melanie, Neil, wake up, we're going fishing. It's time to get up,' says my father in a harsh whisper, shaking me.

I wake up. It is dark. I feel nauseous. 'I feel sick, I don't want to go,' I whine.

'Nonsense. Once you're up catching *palings* – eels – you'll be fine.'

We get up, say nothing, get dressed and stand in a daze. My dad shepherds us out of the room and down the stairs to the car. My dad had put all the fishing tackle and food for the day into the boot of our blue Ford Zephyr the night before.

'What time is it?' I ask.

'Quarter-to-five.'

'It's too early,' I whimper.

'Come on, kids, jump in. We have to pick up the rest of the fishermen and get to the Koonap River on Uncle George McCarthy's farm before the sun comes up so we catch those early-morning feeders. Where's Hendrik? I told him to be on time.'

Just then, Hendrik Swart comes out of the hotel front door, dressed in the same clothes he wears every day, including his suede hat.

'Man, Max, the *paling* fishing should be good today. It was full moon yesterday and there's a light south-easter blowing this morning. As long as the river's dirty, we'll catch 'em, man.'

Hendrik regularly makes predictions about how many fish or eels we will catch. If we don't catch anything, he says something like 'The wind has turned south-west – no good for *palings*. They don't bite in a sou'-wester.'

We drive off and pick up Marie Wessels, who loves fishing and is very good at it, and often catches more than the men. We also pick up Ellie Niewenhuys and Bun Wilson. It is a bit of a tight squeeze. There are eight people in the car – three adults in front on the bench-style seat, two in the back and my brother, my sister and me squeezed into one seat space more or less on top of each other.

We drive down Campbell Street, cross the bridge over the Kat River and head off on the dirt road towards Grahamstown. The morning air is still cool and a faint light appears in the east. The car windows are shut and all five adults light up cigarettes and smoke. Bun starts coughing up phlegm. He opens the window and spits it out. I watch this yellow-green glob fly past my window. That seems to set up a chain reaction and they all start to cough their lungs out. I can't stand the smoke in the car any longer. I can hardly see out the window and can barely breathe and it stinks. I open my window fully. Cold air rushes in and starts to clear the smoke out of the car.

'Close that bloody window, it's freezing!' shouts my father, looking at me in the rear-view mirror.

'Then you stop smoking! I can't breathe,' I complain half under my breath, afraid of being shouted at again.

'Don't be bloody stupid.'

I close my window. When they finish their cigarettes, which they throw out of the window when they get down to the filter, they don't light up again.

'Man, who is going to be the first to catch a *paling* today, Garthie, or will it be a carp or a mullet?' asks Hendrik Swart, trying to lighten up the atmosphere.

'I'm going to catch the first *paling* and a bigger *paling* than you, today, Marie,' Hendrik Swart boasts.

'The only *paling* you will ever catch, Hendrik, is your own, and if you're talking size, you've got no leg to stand on,' replies Marie.

We kids, and probably the adults too, can't wait to hear what is going to come out of Marie's mouth next.

*

The Koonap River, a tributary of the Fish River, runs through George McCarthy's farm. George McCarthy is a big man, like my father, about six foot tall and weighing about two hundred and fifty pounds. Many of my dad's and George's friends are big as well. Often after fishing we go to the farmhouse to visit George.

One unusually cool day in autumn, towards evening, we stop off at the farmhouse before heading home after a fishing trip. A fire is blazing in the hearth and George and a few of his friends are sitting round the fire, each with a brandy in hand. *Oom* Koos, as he is known to everyone, including his family, carefully stuffs his pipe with tobacco, using his huge calloused fingers and puts the pipe into his mouth between his teeth. He then leans forward towards the fire, picks up a red-hot burning coal between his thumb and second and middle fingers, sits back and holds it carefully above his pipe while drawing hard to light the tobacco. He then slowly leans forward again and carefully replaces the coal.

*

We arrive at the Koonap River about an hour later, just before sunrise. The river is flowing gently and the doves are cooing.

After baiting his hook and casting his line into the water, Ellie sits down on a tree stump that is just the right height and distance from the river's edge. All conditions for catching eels are good. Ellie is very optimistic about an excellent day's fishing. We have a perfect spot just under the cliffs where the baboons live. The river is muddy, it is the day after the full moon and there is a light south-easterly breeze.

Ellie lifts his butt to scratch. A minute later he scratches again. We tease him about having ants in his pants, which is what our parents accuse us children of when we don't sit still.

'Man, Marie, I think something is biting my bum!'

'Ellie, I told you long ago to stop working at that nuthouse! How the bloody hell can a tree stump bite your bum?' asks Marie.

Just as Ellie lifts his buttocks off the tree stump to scratch again, a three-foot-long snake darts out of a hole in the top of the stump and slithers off into the bush. Everyone laughs.

The adults fish with rods with reels and we kids fish with a rod that we call a *sweepstok*. It is a six-foot bamboo rod with a piece of string about three to four yards long tied to the top end. The end of the string has a hook and sinker tied onto it. At a variable length along the string, depending on the depth of the water, is a movable float. We often make these floats out of champagne bottle corks painted red with a porcupine quill pierced through the middle of it and threaded onto the line. When a fish or eel starts biting, the cork bobs up and down.

We wait until the cork is dragged under the water, indicating that the fish or eel is hooked and is trying to swim away. Then with a quick action we sweep the rod upwards and the fish or eel comes flying out of the water, quite often over our shoulders, and lands on the ground at the back. To get an eel off the hook, we hold the line in one hand so that the head is just above the ground, with our shoe tramp on the squirming body a little behind the head and pin it on the ground. With the other hand, we take a sharp knife or dagger and pierce it just behind the back of the head, cutting the spinal cord. The eel might give one or two more squirms before dying. Mostly, it is not that easy. An eel could squirm around, get tied up with the line or around one's leg for many minutes before getting it into position to cut the spinal cord. Then the hook can easily be taken out of the mouth.

The next challenge is to skin the eel before we can eat it.

'Garthie, man, the best way to skin a *paling* is to cut off its head, put a fork into the flesh where the head has been cut off, grab the slippery skin with newspaper just behind the fork and pull down towards the tail,' says Hendrik Swart. 'Newspaper is the best, man, for grabbing that slimy skin. And the best way to cook a *paling* is to just fry it on the stove in its own fat.'

He is right. We love eel fried until the white flesh is a crisp brown. It has a stronger taste than other fish.

We go fishing on many of the farms in the area. Since my father is mayor, none of the farmers mind him fishing on their farm, except for Bull Knot, one of the wealthiest cattle farmers in the district. He says he will shoot even his own brother if he catches him fishing on his land.

*

'Oh my god, the boat will sink,' I am convinced as I look at a twenty-feet wall of water in front of me.

The little fishing vessel suddenly sweeps up the face of the wave, hovers at the crest for a few seconds, then plunges forward into a trough that looks like it goes down to the middle of the earth.

'Bwagh.' I retch and spew out more of what must have been the lining of my stomach – there is nothing else left in there to vomit. I look for the land on the horizon, but it is no longer in sight.

The fisherman next to me pulls down his pants, sits with his bum hanging over the edge of the boat, holding on to a metal hook attached to the outside of the engine room, and drops a large brown turd into the sea. Without wiping his arse, he pulls up his pants and drops his line back into the water.

'Which way to shore?' I ask my dad between retches.

He points.

'I'm swimming,' I utter with determination, desperation and conviction.

'I know you're a good swimmer and you'd probably make it to shore, but what about the sharks?'

My heart sinks. I have been on this little fishing boat since five in the morning and will be stuck on it until seven in the evening. The smell of diesel and rotten bait and fish wafts under my nostrils. I can't stand it any longer. I want to die, but I don't want to die in the jaws of a shark.

'It was a really rough sea for a first-time deep-sea fishing trip, Garthie,' says my dad, attempting to comfort me when we finally arrive back at the harbour.

That night and every night for the next week, my bed rocks and rolls and waves of nausea come up from the depths of my stomach. All I can do to stop myself from vomiting is to lie on my back with one arm and one leg hanging over the side of the bed, touching the floor.

'Very few people get seasick a second time, Garthie,' claims my dad six months later.

'Very few people get seasick three times in a row, Garthie,' repeats my dad.

'Very few people get seasick four times in a row, Garthie,' assures my dad again.

On my fifth – yes, fifth and final – deep-sea fishing expedition, I arrive at the docks in the dark with my father at half past four in the morning. I see the little fishing boat bobbing gently up and down in the harbour. As I draw nearer, that familiar smell of diesel mixed with rotten bait and putrid fish remains, immediately triggers intense nausea. My stomach feels like it has already turned inside out and back again. I haven't even stepped on the boat yet.

'Never again! Never again!' I finally gather the courage to scream at my father.

32

Hardship and strife
Not cured by a wand
Silence brings a bond

It is three o'clock on a winter's morning in August. The fire in the middle of Edward Makabane's mud hut had gone out a few hours before. His hut is very sparse. He has a single metal frame bed with springs and a hard coir mattress. On the bed are a few dark brown moth-eaten blankets. He has a few Ship sherry cardboard boxes from the hotel, in which he keeps the few clothes he owns. Edward lives in a small community of about ten huts in the bush. There is no electricity, running water or toilets.

He wakes up shivering. He gets up, goes outside to the communal water tank to get some water to make coffee, opens the tap, but nothing comes out. '*Mnqundu* – arsehole!' he curses aloud to himself.

The water in the tap is frozen again. There is no moon that night, so he has to feel his way around. He takes his knife, digs out a chunk of ice, and manages to get a trickle of water to fill his cup. He lights the fire in his hut again, boils his cup of water and adds a teaspoon of Boereplaas instant coffee and five teaspoons of sugar. He will need that to give him the energy to make the twenty-mile bicycle journey to work by seven o'clock.

'How many more times can I do this every day, every year?' Edward shouts to the sky.

He gets on his bicycle and starts to pedal. There is only the sound of the rusty bicycle chain as it rhythmically squeaks with each turn of the pedal. His beanie covers his ears so that he cannot hear the soft gushing of cold wind, but he can hear the chain squeaking and then, as the dawn's early light starts to break, he can also hear the birds begin to chirp and squawk. He now sees the lights of Fort Beaufort. The last leg is a freewheel down the hill into town, but then, just to make sure life isn't too easy, there is the steep hill up Campbell Street to the hotel.

He rides around the back of the hotel and puts his bicycle in the servants' quarters, where it is safe. His legs are stiff and he struggles a little to start walking up to the kitchen. He gets to the kitchen and sits down at the table next to the pantry where Lena is preparing the bacon for breakfast. Edward is in his mid-thirties. He has a kind face and is always very polite.

'*Jusus, man, Edward, jy lyk uitgepoep. Vat 'n bietjie pap, man* – Jesus, man, Edward, you look pooped out. Have a bit of porridge, man,' says Lena in a very motherly way. Lena is in charge of the pantry. She is very organised. She and her husband live in a small brick-and-mud house in Newtown and have two children.

'*Enkosi* – Thank you,' says Edward. He eats his porridge voraciously, then walks back to the servants' quarters and changes into his waiter's uniform of long black trousers and a maroon jacket.

*

After lunch, my father says I can help Edward bottle wine and sherry. That is one of my favourite jobs. It is always cool and a little damp in the cellar, even when it is 110F in the middle of summer.

I wait at the cellar door.

'*Molo mlungu* – Hello, Master,' says Edward, walking down the courtyard. 'Are you ready to start bottling?'

'*Molo*, Edward. *Ewe* – Yes.'

We have a system well worked out. Edward knocks a thick metal tap into a hole at the top of a large wooden barrel, then swings the vat round, so that the tap is at the bottom. He then puts it on a strong wooden rack sideways, losing only a few drops of wine. He turns on the tap, holding a bottle under it. When it is full, in one movement I pass him an empty bottle and take the full one with the other hand, while he slips the empty one under the running tap. A white ceramic bowl catches any spill. When we have bottled two cases, we stop and bang a cork into each bottle and stick on a wine or sherry label using a creamy paper glue. I know all the wine and sherry labels. I have a scrapbook for school with all the labels we use. Old Brown sherry and sweet muscatel is what we bottle most. That is the cheapest liquor that we mostly sell in the off sales and the 'coloured' bar. The 'white' customers in the bar and ladies lounge mainly drink beer and spirits.

We often bottle until the sun goes down and don't even notice what the time is. We usually speak very little.

Sometimes I say, 'Mmm.'

Fifteen or twenty minutes later, Edward replies, 'Eh.'

These are very special moments for me.

33

A loud thud
Smears of blood
Yet everywhere the law

I hear a thud – a familiar sound on a Saturday afternoon. It is the sound of a body falling onto metal from a height. I cringe again. Often on a Saturday afternoon after a few (or more) drinks at the pub, the police on duty for the weekend drive around the town in their pick-up truck. When they see a drunk 'black' or 'coloured' person, they drive the pick-up at top speed, screech to a halt just in front of the person and jump out. Two or three police officers take an arm and a leg and throw the person as high as they can into the air before he lands in the back of the pick-up. The drunk person then spends the night in gaol. The back of the truck is smeared with patches of old blood.

*

A new police commander comes to town.

'The new police commander says he will not tolerate any monkey business and he's going to run a very tight ship, Ben,' I hear my dad saying to Ben Nel.

They both chuckle.

It is midday on Sunday. Bun Wilson and his wife have come to Deane's for lunch.

'Geography, bring me a number 17 and a gin a tonic for the madam to my table in the dining room,' Bun orders the waiter.

'*Ja, baas,*' says Geography.

On Sundays, the pub opens from midday to two o'clock for customers having Sunday lunch at the hotel. This is a big treat for the townspeople. However, no one is allowed to drink in the bar. They can order drinks from the waiter and drink with their lunch in the dining room or the lounge. Those are the rules. On other days of the week, the bar opens at ten o'clock in the morning, the men drink in the bar, and the women drink in the ladies' lounge. The bar then closes at about ten or eleven o'clock at night.

Once every few months, the provincial police from East London come to Fort Beaufort to make sure that this particular law is being obeyed. The provincial police usually let the local Fort Beaufort commander know when they will be arriving. He then tells my father and the other hotel owners. 'That's how it works,' my dad says.

The provincial police spend a day in town, two or three times a year. They fine people for driving without a license, driving unroadworthy cars, not indicating when they turn a corner, and whatever else they can find.

There is one person the provincial police dread. That person is Dr Sutton. Dr Sutton is eighty-nine years old and still working as a doctor.

I am on my bicycle about to cross the road when I see a young provincial policeman stop Dr Sutton. He has just driven straight through a stop sign, then turned right onto Campbell without indicating, blasting his horn as he turned, so that the oncoming traffic had no choice but to stop for him.

The policeman looks down at the little old man in his almost equally old Morris Minor, and politely says, 'Sir, I must fine you on two…' He doesn't get any further.

Dr Sutton shouts at him, 'Young man, I was here a long time before that stupid stop sign, and when I turn right, everyone in Fort Beaufort knows better than not to stop for me. They are lucky I warn them with my hooter. Now get out of my way and off you go, young man. Can't you see I'm busy?' Dr Sutton drives off in a huff.

The young policeman stands there, staring with his mouth wide open.

34

Rituals of manhood
Change with time
Change the man?

I can barely see over the podium at age thirteen. I am dressed in a black suit, white shirt and a tie. I can almost see my reflection in my black shiny shoes. Next to me in Temple Hillel in East London stands Rabbi Shonfeld.

*

Reverend Benjamin Sass, who we call Benjy behind his back, initially tutors me for my bar mitzvah. He is large in every respect, tall, has a big mouth and a loud voice. He walks duck-footed with a slightly backward stoop. Every time he sees me, he bellows at the top of his voice in front of everyone, 'Alperstein, have you been reading the Bible?'

'No,' I answer honestly.

'Then you're an ignoramus!' he bellows back.

Benjy is a reverend because he has not passed his rabbi exams yet. After a year, he leaves to do further studies on his way to becoming a rabbi and is replaced by Rabbi Shonfeld, a small man with a full beard and quietly spoken – the very opposite of Benjy.

It has taken two years of preparation. I have had to attend Friday night and Saturday morning services, and spend an hour after every Saturday morning service learning to read Hebrew. I have to conduct both services and read from the Torah – the holy scrolls – in Hebrew. Learning to read

Hebrew is daunting enough, but the Torah, which is handwritten, has no vowel symbols attached to the letters to help with pronunciation. At least I have a good meal of roast lamb and roast potatoes after every Friday night service with my Uncle Hilly and Aunt Kitty Cooper and my cousins David, Peter, Linda and Dianne.

Following the Saturday morning service, David Berman and I catch a bus downtown and have a waffle at the Wimpy Bar or a plate of soggy chips with salt and vinegar. If we are caught, we will be caned. We are supposed to return to the boarding school straight after the service and our bar mitzvah lesson. We are never caught, which is difficult to understand, since we are dressed in our full school uniform, including straw bashers. The only children who would be wearing a school uniform on a Saturday would be boarders. We stick out like sore thumbs. There are a few consolations to this painful passage to manhood.

*

Behind me is a large decorated wooden structure closed off with thick blue curtains, behind which is the Torah. I am about to conduct the entire Friday evening service in Hebrew. The day of my bar mitzvah has finally arrived. It is the day I am supposed to change from a boy to a man. I will now be accepted into the congregation of men, be expected to behave like a man, and be counted to make up a *minyan* – quorum – for a service.

I look down at all the people gathered to hear the bar mitzvah service. My mother, the atheist, and my father, the agnostic, sit there looking more nervous than I am feeling. I can read the Hebrew fluently, but don't have a clue what it all means. The only task is one of deciphering the letters. I read without error in both the Friday evening and Saturday morning services.

*

It is the year 1940. A seventeen-year-old Xhosa boy sits in the cattle kraal near eBofolo with his father. He chews at the boiled foreleg of a goat that each umkwetha – initiate-to-be into manhood – has been given to eat. It does not taste very good – all the fat has been cut off. He has to finish it.

His head is shaved and he is given a necklace made from the tail of one of his father's cows. A new sheepskin kaross is wrapped around his broad shoulders. Next to him are a knobkierie and an assegai. He will need those when living on his own in the bush for six weeks, away from his tribe.

That evening he and all the abakwetha – initiates – dance all night with the young girls of the tribe. They are all naked. He watches some of the young girls' breasts shaking as they dance in the moonlight. He knows he has to be honourable. He will only dance until the sun rises in the morning.

*

The sun is up. The air is still. He stands motionless in front of a large flat rock. It is near where the two rivers meet. eBofolo is visible in the distance. In his head is a silent scream, outside is the sound of the assegai blade cutting flesh and scraping on stone. He had imagined how the pain might be, but he was wrong. He dares not flinch nor utter a sound. He does not want to bring shame on his father, his family or himself.

'You are now a man,' shouts the incibi – circumciser – as he throws the piece of skin to the ground. He wraps leaves around the bleeding area of the penis and then smears on mud. His entire body is painted white with clay from the cliffs near a cave, and a blanket is wrapped around him.

The young man picks up the foreskin off the ground and carefully walks over to the nearest anthill, where he buries it, so that the ants can eat it. The witchdoctor must not find the skin. The witchdoctor can make dangerous medicine from it.

He picks up his assegai and knobkierie, turns around to look at his family and walks off into the bush.

35

Of a life gone too soon
What never was said
In silence remains

'Wake up, Alperstein. Wake up.' Mr Barker, the principal of Selbourne College High School, stands in his checked dressing gown, shaking me by the shoulder.

I look up at him, wondering why he would have come all the way from his house to the boarding house.

'Your uncle is coming to pick you up in fifteen minutes to take you home for the weekend.'

It is Saturday, 13 March.

'Excuse me, sir, what is the time, sir?'

'It is five o'clock, Alperstein. Now get up. Your uncle will be here shortly. Just pack a few clothes and your toiletries.'

I get dressed, pack a little suitcase and go downstairs to wait for my uncle. He arrives. My brother and sister are sitting in the back, looking dazed. They have expressions on their faces I have never seen before. I frown, puzzled.

'Garthie, do you know why we're going to Fort Beaufort?' asks my Uncle Hilley with a look on his face that I have also not seen before.

I feel very uneasy. Something is wrong.

'No. Mr Barker said I was going home for the weekend.' I now know that something is very wrong. I feel scared.

'Your father died last night. He had a massive heart attack.'

The blood drains from my head. I feel dizzy. I put my head between my legs. I think I am going to faint.

'I knew he died. I woke up at the time he died, and just couldn't go to sleep again,' says Melanie.

Neil just sits, looking pale and bewildered. He is five years younger than me. He is only ten years old.

36

The innocence of youth
Whittled away
Lost

My seventeenth birthday comes and goes. After my childhood, birthdays don't play a particularly prominent place in my life.

'Garth, you should at least get your licence. You can now drive legally,' teases my mother.

I drive round to Frik van Wyk's office. He is responsible for issuing drivers' licences. I park the car outside and walk in. '*Goeie môre, Meneer van Wyk* – Good morning, Mr van Wyk. Can I please get my driver's licence, Meneer van Wyk?' I ask politely.

'What! Have you been driving all these years without a licence? If you weren't late Max's son…' He stops short, shaking his head sadly. 'Well, go for a drive around the block while I do all the paperwork. *Vok die duiwel* – Fuck the devil,' I hear him mutter under his breath as I leave the office.

I drive around the block and collect my driver's licence.

*

It is school holidays a year before. 'Smoky' Robinson, Alan McComb, Yolanda Duplessis, her brother Phillip, Michael Minty and I walk down Campbell Street. We are on our way to visit Debbie Dressel at the Royal Hotel near the other end of Campbell Street, opposite the butcher shop. When I was younger, I loved the smell of raw meat, and every time I walked past the butcher, I would stick my nose in for a sniff. Yolanda's father owns the butcher shop. Yolanda has a bit of a crush on Alan. He isn't quite sure what to do about it so, for the time being, hangs out with us all.

I am wearing my pink and white-striped Bermuda shorts, no shirt, and an African bead necklace around my throat. The others are wearing plain T-shirts and very short shorts. We are all barefoot. As we pass Audrey Delponte's clothes shop, I see my mother and Audrey sitting and chatting. I linger in the doorway. They are both smoking cigarettes and have filled the shop with a haze of cigarette smoke.

'Did you hear about that kid Colin Brown, Rose? He set a dog alight and threw it off the Settlers Bridge into the Kat River. He's only eight. I heard he's been sent to a reform school.'

'Did you hear about the Sinclair boy, Audrey?'

'No.'

'He was found dead with a bag over his head attached to the exhaust pipe of his car in his garage. What a shame. He was only thirty.'

'Why did he do that?'

My mother leans over, looks around her, and whispers to Audrey, 'Homosexual.' Seeing me eavesdropping on their conversation, she yells, 'Put on a bloody shirt.'

'I have a beautiful pink-collared shirt and really cool black leather pants that will fit you just perfectly,' says Audrey.

'Audrey still trying to get you into leather pants, Garth?' asks Smoky.

'*Ja*, but you wouldn't catch me dead in leather pants. Not in a million years.'

We walk past the BP garage where Koos Wessels is working in the spares. He is doing a holiday job.

'Hey, Fathead, stop sitting on your arse and do some bloody work,' yells Alan.

'*Hey, vok jou* – fuck you,' replies Koos, with a smirk on his face. 'Don't go and get pissed at the Royal now, hey.'

When we reach the Royal, Debbie is sitting in the lounge. She is a few years younger than the rest of us, has long dark-brown hair that is parted down the middle, and has a pretty face. Many of the young blokes around town are checking her out.

'How 'bout we get a few beers?'

'*Ja*, OK, but we better sit in the back lounge,' says Debbie. 'My dad could get into trouble serving alcohol to us. What do you want?'

'I'll have a number 17.'

'*Ja*, me too,' pipes up everyone else.

'Actually, no, I don't want a Lion lager, I'll have a Castle, thanks, Debbie,' says Alan.

Debbie disappears to the bar and returns with a young African waiter.

'Your beers, Baases and Madams.'

'*Enkosi* – Thank you, Patio,' says Phillip, who speaks fluent Xhosa. He grew up on a farm.

'How the hell did he get the name Patio, Debbie?' asks Michael when the waiter has left.

'Buggered if I know,' says Debbie.

We sit there with our legs crossed, trying to look very adult as we gulp down our beers.

'Are you going to the bop on Saturday night at the Scout hall? Mum Doodle and the Kraansburgers are playing.'

'*Ja*, of course.'

'Hey, why don't you drink up and let's go up to Deane's and play a bit of music. My guitar's up there,' says Smoky.

We walk up the hill to Deane's a little light-headed and giggling, and on the opposite side of the road to Audrey's shop to avoid my mother and Audrey. Smoky gets his guitar from my room and we go to the back of the hotel, to the sample room, where we can make a noise and not be heard. We sit on the floor, a little dozy by now, and listen to Smoky strum his guitar and sing one of his favourite songs – 'Whisky and Rye', by Donovan. Smoky is totally besotted with Donovan, a 1960s Irish folk singer. None of us can believe that Donovan's dad would actually introduce him at his concerts – 'Wending my way through the flowers here, I'd like to introduce my son – the phenomenon of Donovan!' – he said on the Donovan LP in the thickest of Irish accents. We think that is very cool. It is the age of flower power and hippies, which our parents don't like at all.

*

Saturday night arrives. The temperature hasn't cooled down much from 105F. The Scout hall is packed with all the teens of the town and the music is blaring at a volume incompatible with hearing someone shouting right into your ear. Some are dressed in their best going out clothes, the boys with their hair slicked back with Brylcreem, and others in T-shirts and shorts, and barefoot.

'You're not going to the dance in a T-shirt and those horrible Bermuda shorts of yours, Garth, and put some bloody shoes on!' shouts my mother as I walk past the reception.

The dance of the moment is an imitation (as best we can) of the British twist of the early 60s. In between songs, boys and girls stand opposite each other, awkwardly waiting for the next song to begin, so that they can start twisting again, or coyly hold hands.

'Hey, Garth, check: Yolanda grabbed Mac's hand. He looks so *skaam* – shy,' shouts Smoky into my ear.

Mum Doodle and the Kraansburgers have a drummer, a lead guitarist, a bass guitarist and a singer. Their hair is shiny black with all the Brylcreem and wear very short shorts and sandals. They play mainly modern pop music. Their favourite tune, one that they play repeatedly, is by Tony Orlando and Dawn. With the thickest Fort Beaufort accent, they sing, 'Knock thrree taams on the ceiling if you wa'ant mee…'

Sweat pours and bodies gyrate for hours as if in a trance. By one o'clock in the morning, there is usually a fight outside the Scout hall, which is either broken up by the adults in charge at the bop or the police if many are involved in the brawl. Parents are sometimes called. What happens to their children behind closed doors at home is nobody else's business.

*

Golf is another favourite pastime. I started playing golf when I was about ten years old. Fort Beaufort's golf course is on the north side of town in the direction of Healdtown next to the airport. The airport runway doubles as one of the fairways of the golf course. Light aircraft such as Cessnas can land there. We play mainly during the week outside of the official playing times. I have a few second-hand clubs that we share. Most of the fairways are dry dirt or patchy grass, but the greens are well kept.

'Garth, I've had some complaints from the golf club again. You and your brother and your friends were seen playing golf wearing T-shirts and slip-slops. You know the dress regulation is a proper shirt, proper shoes and socks up to your knees,' says my mom, sounding somewhat frustrated.

'But Mom, it was Tuesday morning. We were the only ones on the golf course. No one else other than the bloke who does the greens would have seen us.'

'Sorry, those are the rules. That's what your father would have said.'

*

During holidays, we also while away our time driving to nearby towns – Alice, Adelaide, Bedford and sometimes as far as Somerset East to have tea and scones or instant coffee and anchovy toast. The conversation usually goes like this.

'Mom, can I take the car? We want to go to Alice.'

'It's another year till you get your licence. You bloody better be careful. Anyway, why can't you have your bloody tea and scones at Kouvaras Café?'

'We've got nothing to do.'

'You kids make me sick. That's all you have to say – nothing to do! What can I do now? OK, take the bloody car, but be careful.'

Melanie, Neil, Koos Wessels, Smoky Robinson and I get into my mother's powder-blue Ford Anglia and head off to Alice. We pass the dry river beds where we used to spend many hours playing as young children, and pass Red Hill, covered with aloes. I wonder whether it is called Red Hill because of all the aloes and their bright spear-like red flowers sticking above the fleshy green leaves, or whether there had been a bloody battle there between the Xhosas and the British.

The heat shimmers above the road and occasionally a mirage appears.

We reach Alice in about twenty minutes. Alice looks like a smaller version of Fort Beaufort. We drive past the local pub to the only café in town. I park the car outside the café. We get out and head in. We are the only customers.

A young 'coloured' waitress approaches us. She is probably about sixteen years old. She is wearing a white apron and a little white embroidered hat. She places a menu down on the table. The choices are Pitco Tips tea, Koffiehuis instant coffee, anchovy toast, toast with Marmite or scones with jam and cream.

'*Wat wil julle hê* – What do you want?'

'Can we have five coffees and five anchovy toasts please?'

'*Suiker met die koffie* – Sugar with the coffee?'

'*Ja, twee* – Yes, two.'

We always ordered the same thing at the Alice café. They made good anchovy toast – a lot of butter soaked into hot toast and lots of that salty anchovy fish paste.

I become uncomfortable looking at the young girl. It suddenly dawns on me that in all our café crawling, we have never been served by a white teenager. I sit quietly, eating my anchovy toast and drinking my Koffiehuis coffee. We leave her a tip. Two cents. What can that buy? Two little lollies.

'You're being very quiet,' says Koos as I drive back to Fort Beaufort.

'Yes.'

37

The Beatles
And cigarettes
Young old Eric

'Is he going to Cape Town University?' I overhear one of the customers in the bar enquire of Eric Delponte, filling in behind the counter as barman.

'Yes,' answers Eric with a knowing smirk.

'*Nog 'n donder se kommie, nê* – Another bloody communist, right?'

'*Ja*, he'll come back with long hair, beard, tie-dye T-shirts and talking all that *Kaffir-boetie* communist propaganda shit. Just you watch, hey,' says another customer.

*

After my father died in 1965, when I was fifteen-years of age, our GP, Dr Jan Dippenaar, became a father figure and role model to me. He was a very calm, considered and compassionate person who treated 'coloured' and 'black' patients for free. He had a separate surgery for them, as was the practice, but treated them with respect. He began to take me to the Fort Beaufort 'black' hospital on his ward rounds and let me assist at minor operations. I very soon thereafter decided I wanted to be a doctor.

'Why don't you rather do chemical engineering?' asked my mother when I told her I wanted to do medicine. 'You like science and chemistry.'

For a number of years I had toyed with the idea of becoming a motor mechanic. My mother's response was 'You want to spend the rest of your life with dirty black grease under your fingernails? Forget it!'

I had worked in Dolfie van der Decken's garage as an apprentice during a number of school holidays and loved fixing cars. I was assigned to work with a Xhosa man named Edward. He was a short man, very strong and always had a mischievous smile. He had a very wicked sense of humour and would often mimic Dolfie and the other 'white' mechanics. He did not speak English very well, but he knew all the swear words. If he accidentally hurt himself he would utter 'Cunt! *Poes*! *Moer*!' obviously mimicking the 'whites', and practically kill himself laughing.

My motor mechanic experience stood me in good stead when I bought my first car at university and had little money. I was able to do all my services, engine tuning and most repairs. I finally handed over to the professionals when motorcars were made with fuel injection systems and were tuned using computerised methods – beyond my skills.

During my last year of high school I applied to the medical schools of the University of Cape Town and Witwatersrand University in Johannesburg. I was accepted by both universities but chose to go to Cape Town.

*

Eric had lived most of his life in Port Elizabeth. He worked in the advertising section of the Port Elizabeth *Herald*.

'Charlie Lee, the only Chinese person on the staff, and I used to meet for breakfast every morning before work. Breakfast was always anchovy toast and coffee,' says Eric.

How Eric ever found himself in Fort Beaufort is a mystery. He is fifty, but a very young fifty. He dresses very tastefully, is always well groomed, speaks with a refined English South African accent and loves Beatles music. His favourite album is *Abbey Road* and his favourite tune 'Come Together'. He knows the words to all the songs. Eric is married to Audrey, who owns the clothing shop next to Millards. He rents a small space next to Kouvaras Café where he sells cigarettes and sweets and listens to Beatles music.

'Eric doesn't even earn enough to buy the bloody cigarettes,' complains Audrey.

Eric's space, which doesn't have a name, is the hangout for the teenagers of the town. We spend endless hours discussing the Beatles, the Rolling Stones, Black Sabbath and all the new rock bands that most parents hate with a passion or have never heard of. I think Eric prefers the company of teenagers to his own age group. He is either still stuck in adolescence or going through a second one. Whichever, he is a misfit in Fort Beaufort.

*

'You lucky bum, you'll have a ball at Cape Town University. Boy, do I envy you, you bum,' says Eric affectionately.

38

Hold down
Cold concrete walls
Black man, convulse!

Fort Beaufort had the largest mental institution in the Southern hemisphere for 'black' people only. As young children, my brother, my sister, friends and I used to ride our bicycles all around the town and would often stop at one of the sections of the hospital, surrounded by a high barbed-wire fence, where a particular patient whom we had nicknamed George Paraffin resided. We used to tease and taunt him with that name until he chased us and sometimes threw things at us. We were never reprimanded for our behaviour.

Every Christmas, a thousand mental patients were guided through the streets of Fort Beaufort, singing Christmas carols for the amusement and entertainment of the 'white' residents of the town. They were dressed in grey pyjama-like clothes, some with white stripes that were reminiscent of prison uniforms. A few wore colourful beanies on their heads. They were surrounded on all sides by the hospital orderlies and burly guards in brown uniforms and pith helmets.

We used to watch from the balcony of the second storey of the hotel. We were too scared to go downstairs. George Paraffin might see us and chase us.

*

In my first year at medical school, during my June holiday, Ellie

Niewenhuys asked me whether I would like to visit the mental hospital and see what work he did.

I meet him at the main entrance to the hospital on Somerset Street near the Fort Beaufort Primary School. He is dressed in his usual uniform, which consists of a wrinkled charcoal black suit, a white shirt and a black hat.

'Blarry cold this morning hey, Garthie.'

'*Ja*, Ellie, it's very cold. There's still frost on the ground. This morning a chunk of ice came out of the tap when I opened it.'

We walk into a cold room. The walls are bare cement and the room smells of cold damp and hospital disinfectant. In the middle is an electric machine next to a leather-covered table.

The psychiatrist is an older Italian man. Six 'black' nurses bring a young 'black' man into the room on a stretcher.

'Watch this, man. I bet you've never seen this before.' says Ellie.

'You can'a bet on'a it,' says the psychiatrist with a very strong Italian intonation and lets out a loud sardonic cackle.

The man lies on the bare leather table on his back. He looks very scared. No one says anything to him. One of the nurses puts electrodes on his head. Five others firmly hold his limbs. A nurse puts a rubber guard into his mouth between his teeth and tells him to bite.

'In a "white"a hospital it is done'a a little differentaly'a,' continues the psychiatrist. 'The patient is given'a anaesthetic and paralysed'a. You don't see'a any of this'a.' He repeats his laugh as he turns on and off a switch on the machine connected by wires to the man's head.

The man's body starts to twitch, his limbs and head started to jerk rhythmically, his eyes roll backwards, then his whole body convulses violently. The five nurses struggle to hold him down. After about two minutes, which feels like about two hours to me, the convulsing decreases in intensity and finally stops. I feel a bit dizzy and nauseous. The image of a thousand patients from the mental hospital running in the streets singing Christmas carols in English and Xhosa flashes before my eyes.

39

The mountain gave refuge
Suffering and war
Also love

I am ready. I have my guitar, backpack with a few clothes, toothbrush, hairbrush and swimming cossie. The bus, with Hobbiton-on-Hoggsback written on the side, pulls up outside Deane's. I jump on.

'Hi, Peter. Got a full bus of kids from Port Elizabeth, have you? And quite a few new "aunties" as well?'

'Yes. It's freezing up at Hoggsback. There's snow already. There'll be a lot of work for you and John. You learner doctors will have your hands full this winter.'

From my second year of medical school, I volunteered at Hobbiton-on-Hoggsback, a camp for under-privileged 'white' children. There were no such camps for 'black' children. My classmate and friend, John Fletcher, had been going there for a number of years. We were mainly there to look after the young kids, but we were also the unofficial 'doctors' and treated all the sick kids. Occasionally a child had to be taken to the GP in Alice.

*

We drive through Alice, past Chief Sandile's Kop, which is where Fort Hare University is now located, cross the Tyhume river near Chief Tyali's Great Place and can see Chief Gaika's Kop to the north. Young 'black' children, barefoot and wearing tattered jerseys and shorts, run towards us holding up oxen and wild pigs made with clay and painted with white limestone. They are hoping to sell them. There are snow patches here and there.

We finally reach the camp in the Amatola mountains. I recognise many of the other 'aunties' and 'uncles'. There is Jon, who used to be a Springbok swimmer; Kathy and Sharon; Rob who is a schoolteacher and also went to Selbourne College.

'Who's that new auntie there with the bloody kaffir beads around her neck? How ridiculous!' Rob blurts in a loud voice followed by a guffaw and a few snorts.

I look at her. Other than his racism, there is something else I am reacting to. I keep looking at her. I don't quite know what it is. I have never felt like that before.

'I don't see anything wrong with those beads. I like bead necklaces.'

'Come on, have a bottle of golden nectar, as we call it here.' A bottle of Lion lager was thrust into my face followed by another guffaw and a snort.

'No thanks, not now, maybe later.'

I can't stop looking at her. 'Hello, my name's Garth. Have you been to Hobbiton before?'

'I'm Melissa. I saw you getting on the bus in Fort Beaufort with your guitar. No, this is my first time.'

Our eyes meet.

40

Flying saucers
Stories to tell
In famous Fort Beaufort

On the day after Neil's seventeenth birthday on 26 June 1972, he comes running into the courtyard. 'A UFO has landed in Fort Beaufort – on Bennie Smit's farm! A UFO, a UFO, a UFO!' he repeats. Being into 'space travel', he is in his element.

'Another Eartherland story, and even at age seventeen,' I say to Melanie, rolling my eyes.

'No, it's true,' he insists.

Soon the story is all over town. Everyone is talking about it.

'Mom, did you hear what happened? Piet Kitching tried to shoot the flying saucer. You know, the young blond policeman,' says Neil, very excited.

'After how many beers? What an idiot,' replies my mother quite nonchalantly as she blows a stream of smoke upwards through the nicotine stained yellow streak in her hair. 'Now leave me in peace. I'm trying to work out all this metric stuff. Why we've had to switch to bloody metric when even England and America haven't, God alone knows! I don't know how the 'blacks' are ever going to get it right.'

In the bar, the stories grow more and more elaborate.

'Did you hear about the flying saucer that landed on Smit's farm? It was from outer space and aliens came out and tried to attack the labourers,' claims George Johns.

'*Kak storie, blaai om* – Shit story, turn over [the page],' growls Gerrie

Potgieter. 'That's not what happened. It landed, had flashing yellow lights, turned from grey to bright green, then turned red like a fire ball and then just disappeared.'

'Bullshit,' says Paul van Rensburg. 'It was first a red ball of fire, then turned bright green, then turned yellow-white and Piet Kitching and Bennie Smit shot at it with a double-barrel shotgun and the aliens fired back. Piet and Bernie ducked and they missed. Lucky.'

'It washn't a bloody double-barrelled shotgun. Don't you know your fuggin' gunsh. It wash a fuggin' .303 rifle, idiot,' drawls Harry Els.

'I think they just had too much fuckin' *poeswyn* – cheap wine,' cut in George.

Everyone and their dog wants to visit the site, including us. We drive out along the dirt road to the farm, but the army had come from Grahamstown and cordoned off the area. So there is nothing to see other than dry land scattered with mimosa thorn trees.

*

A common version of the story, as it evolved, was that early that morning Boer de Klerk, one of the 'coloured' labourers on Bennie Smit's farm Braeside, saw an oval red ball of fire hovering above a tree. The red ball turned green and then yellow-white and was shooting out flames. Bennie Smit found him and three other labourers hiding in a shed terrified. Smit then went for his rifle and called the police. He returned and fired eight shots at the object, which then disappeared. When Sergeant Piet Kitching and Commander Philip van Rensburg arrived, the UFO had disappeared. As they were about to leave, a dark grey metal oval object emerged above the thorn trees. Both Kitching and Smit fired at it with their .303 rifles, but the bullets just bounced off. It then suddenly disappeared leaving nine circular 'footprints' ten centimetres across and about twenty-five centimetres deep.

*

'Rose, did you hear they sent the soil from the footprints to be analysed, but it's been lost,' says Audrey to my mother sitting in the ladies' lounge with a gin and tonic in her hand, and tries to disguise her laughter behind her other hand.

'Typical bloody incompetence of our police,' chortles my mother.

'I heard the government intercepted the shipment. Top secret, classified information, you know. Don't tell anyone I said that,' whispers Pam Reynolds, looking around the lounge to see who all might have heard her.

'Don't worry, Pam, even the BBC knows that, and they're having interviews with Bennie Smit and Piet Kitchings and making fools of them. I heard it on LM Radio. The good thing is that now even people in England have heard of Fort Beaufort. Before that, even people in Cape Town didn't know that Fort Beaufort existed,' says Audrey emptying her glass.

41

> A mother to me
> But it cannot be
> The heart hangs heavy

'How do you bear this heat?' asks Melissa. Her parents have allowed her to visit me in Fort Beaufort for a week during the Christmas holidays, chaperoned by a younger sister, Josephine.

'It's only 40C today,' I say. 'Let's go to the cottage.' I want to introduce you to Beauty, my old nanny. She's in Fort Beaufort for a few days.'

We walk past the cellar and turn left through the short passage to the cottage at the back of the hotel.

In one of the rooms, Beauty is sitting next to a table. She immediately looks at Melissa. '*Ngubani lowo* – Who is that?' she says.

'*Igama lakhe ngu Melissa* – Her name is Melissa,' I reply.

Beauty stands, steps back, looks her up and down a number of times, stares at her face and into her eyes. She then turns her gaze to me. '*Uzotshata nini* – When are you getting married?'

I had her approval and permission.

*

Beauty now lives in a mud hut about twenty kilometres outside Fort Beaufort in a small community similar to Edward, the waiter's. When Melanie, Neil and I were all in boarding school, my mother said she was no longer able to afford to keep her on staff at the hotel. During a university holiday, Melissa and I visit her. Scrawny chickens come running in and out of the hut and I can hear pigs grunting outside. Her hut has mud walls with three holes about thirty centimetres square as windows, and a rectangular doorway (with no door) about a metre and a half high. The roof is made from straw. The floor inside the hut has been smoothed with cow dung.

To the left there is a single bed frame with an old coir mattress and a blanket with many threadbare patches. Beauty sleeps on the bed. William, her first grandchild, sleeps on a mat on the floor. She has one wooden chair next to the fire in the middle of the hut. The pervading smell of the hut is smoke from mimosa wood burned for cooking and to keep warm. The dried cow dung has no odour. There are six other huts on about two acres of land. They look just like Beauty's hut.

Two huts are painted with limestone whitewash halfway up the wall, to just below the small windows. There are a few mimosa thorn trees scattered about, but no shade trees. The land, with large eroded *dongas*, slopes down to a small stream about half a kilometre from the huts. A few malnourished dogs, many scrawny chickens and a thin pig scrounge around for scraps of food and insects.

Melissa and I sit next to Beauty on her bed. She lights a fire under a three-legged black pot with water in it. When it boils, she scoops up the boiling water into an old metal teapot with tea leaves. She pours the tea into two chipped china teacups and hands them to us on saucers. There are five other people in the hut, who are sitting on the floor. They are an older man of about seventy-five, a woman of similar age, two young men in their twenties and a teenage girl. It is the middle of June and it is cold. Over their torn frayed secondhand clothes, probably from the Anglican Church in Fort Beaufort, they are wrapped in frayed, thin brown blankets.

'Thet bleddy Dutchman, he know nothing,' shouts Beauty.

The others in the room snigger.

'I told him – you try to touch my land, I kill you, old as I em.'

'What the magistraat he say, *makhulu*?' asks one of the older men.

'He just laugh, the bleddy raw Dutchman. He know nothing.'

'Then I go to the doctor. He says, "Beauty, go ahhh," and he puts a stick down my throat.'

'And what you do, Beauty?' asks the old man again.

'I open my mouth wide, stick out my tongue, like this, and go ahhhhh. And he says, "Go ahhhh again, Beauty." I say I already went ahhhhh enough. Just give me the medicine or I go to *igqira* – witchdoctor!'

That statement is followed by a long cackle from the old man. Everyone in the hut follows with loud laughter, some holding their abdomens they are laughing so much.

'Beauty, I have to go now. Can I bring you anything the next time I come to visit you?' I ask.

'Just some flour and sugar, thank you.'

I look in disbelief. What else could she say – a house in Fort Beaufort, an education, a well-paying job, equality, respect, the vote? I cry all the way home.

*

Beauty died in the same poverty in which she grew up, plagued by arthritis for which she could not afford any treatment. I never knew or ever found out where she was born, who her parents were, what kind of a life she lived before she took the job as my nanny. I didn't even know her Xhosa name or who her husband was. I don't know where she is buried. I learned of her death two years after she died.

42

> Away from her children
> Away from her home
> She passes alone

New York, 1983. It is early evening. The phone rings.

'Hello. Garth.'

'Hi, this is Melanie.'

'Howzit? What's up?'

'The Queen has been admitted to Groote Schuur Hospital again. Diabetes, out of control – again. But don't come flying back. Her doctor, Peter Chapman, remember him? – he was a year or two behind you at UCT – he said he'll be discharging her in a couple of days.'

'OK. Give her my love then.'

Over the past twenty years, the Queen had suffered three heart attacks and one stroke. She smoked through all the heart attacks, but finally stopped after her stroke. Her smoking hand was paralysed. That was two years ago, and she didn't take up smoking again when she recovered from the stroke. I wondered whether the addiction centre in her brain had been affected by the stroke.

I don't sleep well.

'Lissa, I'm flying back to Cape Town on the first flight I can get.'

'But Melanie said your mother would be discharged in a day or two.'

'I know.'

I phone to book a flight to Cape Town. 'The soonest you have. Tomorrow afternoon? Thank you.'

The phone rings in the wee hours of the morning. I fumble for the phone, drop it and pick it up. 'Hello, who is it?'

'This is your Uncle Hilley. I have bad news for you, Garthie. Your mother died. I'm sorry, is it the middle of the night for you? I got the time difference wrong. She died at eight o'clock last night. I'm sorry, I should have called you then, but I figured out the time wrong.'

That was when I called Pan Am. On my father's birthday, 28 August.

*

The old San woman knows what is happening. She knows she is getting closer to the ancestors of her people. She knows her mind is here and then it is there. She hears the children's voices. The voices fade into the distance. Her vision becomes blurred, then clear, then blurred again.

The time has come. She knows what she has to do. In the distance, she sees a young girl playing in a puddle of water after a big rain. It is her. She smiles. Her eyes close slightly as a series of events race through her head. Like a moving picture, she envisions the first time she kisses her husband and he touches her breast, then suddenly she is giving birth to her first child. She stands near the big aloe tree. The pain is intense, but like her mother and her mother before her had done, she knows how to bear the pain and be silent, before her baby slides down between her legs in a gush of yellow fluid and blood. She has not known such joy, such happiness, such love. Her children run before her eyes one after the other, through their ages and stages into adulthood and then her grandchildren appear before her.

Her husband comes back from a hunt with his bow and pack of arrows over one shoulder and a deer over the other; then another one and another one. Then she sees him on the ground, shaking and shivering, turning paler by the day. He develops a rash all over his body. He can neither stand nor move. She starts to feel sad. They all know. Now she knows.

The sun is falling below the sky past the baobab tree. The horizon turns bright red, almost luminous. She picks up her two sticks. She pulls herself to a standing position and slowly, one painful step at a time, makes her way past the sleeping shelters, past the mimosa thorn trees and walks and walks until she is deep into the night and can stagger no more.

She lies down on the cold earth, clutches her sticks close to herself and looks at all the stars in the sky for the last time. She closes her eyes. There is darkness. There is silence. The wind blows away her footprints.

43

Memories of past
Tomorrow gone
Rebirth

It is 1993; three years after Nelson Mandela is released from jail.

'I went to visit Shirley this year in Fort Beaufort. It's a very different Fort Beaufort from what you remember, Garth,' says Smoky, who I am visiting in Tasmania. 'It's now like any African town. There are people everywhere, on the footpaths, in the streets. Everything now happens on the street. They're selling goods, walking, talking and sleeping in the street. You can't drive a car more than ten kilometres an hour through town. There's barely a white face to be seen. Shirley said I should drive with the doors locked and windows rolled up. The buildings are dilapidated and there's garbage everywhere.'

*

Not long after Smoky's visit, in March 1994, Deane's Commercial Hotel burned down. Neil was quite upset by the news. He still had fond memories of his childhood in the hotel. Melanie said it was like a true break with the past, which was sad, but symbolically exciting since it occurred about the same time as the first democratic elections. My feelings were similar to Melanie's. There was a short report in *The Daily Dispatch* and *Die Beeld*, which stated that the fire might have been due to an electrical fault or started by a cigarette butt. Some speculated it was arson for insurance.

*

'*Auk! Hayi! Uthixo ophezulu* – God above!' shouts Edward.

He and Geography just stare at each other. They are sitting on the riverbank, near where the Kat joins the Brak. Their heads keep nodding from side to side.

The expression on their faces is a combination of disbelief and ecstasy. The sound of shrill voices can be heard ululating across the sky of Fort Beaufort. Their time has come. It is 10 May 1994. Nelson Mandela is sworn in as President of the Republic of South Africa.

*

It is January 1996. My family, Melanie, her son Batandwa and Neil drive up to the centre of town. Almost all the people I see are Xhosa or Khoikhoi or mixed-race-looking. There is a token 'white' face to be seen here and there. We go looking for Alperstein Street. When my father died, not only did the fortnightly Fort Beaufort *Advocate* devote an entire issue to him, but also the Fort Beaufort Council elected to name a street after him. They chose the street leading to the sewage purification plant, presumably because he was responsible for upgrading the town's sewage system. They also misspelt his name – Alpertstein Street, it was called.

After a long search in the area where I think it must be, I ask one of the locals near the sewerage plant.

'I don't know. All the street signs have disappeared in the past few years.'

'I'm sure it's this street alongside the sewage plant. That looks and smells like a sewage treatment plant to me,' says Melanie.

I look up Alpertstein Street on Google Maps – it is precisely where Melanie thinks it is.

'What happened to Lena, Katy, Mickie, and Sakkie and Tollie, all the "coloured" people from the hotel?' I ask an older 'coloured' man, with a wizened face in the Newtown township.

Newtown is even more run down than Fort Beaufort.

'*Hulle is almal dood* – They are all dead,' replies the old man with a sad look.

*

My whole family spend the day visiting our old haunts. We run across both swing bridges. The one below the Fort Beaufort museum is in good shape, and the other near Roger Crane's parents' house is a little rickety, but passable. The Martello tower is surrounded by litter and smells like a toilet. Dion, our eldest son, calls us over to look at a snakeskin in front of the door to the tower. We crouch down to look at it and see the snakeskin, probably a cobra's, transparent with age, and inside it a dried-out lizard. Melissa makes a sketch of it.

The barrage where we used to see the *likkewaans* is overflowing like a mini Niagra Falls. I have never seen Fort Beaufort so green and lush, with the Kat River almost overflowing its banks. An old man says he has never seen so much rain in Fort Beaufort as in the past few months – ever!

'Daddy, you said Fort Beaufort's in the desert,' complains Dion, our ten-year-old.

'Yes, you said there'd be dry cracked ground and scorpions and snakes,' his six-year-old brother, Lucien, joins in.

*

It is January 2010. Neil, his wife Eli and their two young children Amelie and Sofia, Melanie and I once again stand in front of the town hall looking across the street at where Deane's Hotel used to be. Andrew Stevens, a friend of Neil's and the son of the late principal of the primary school we went to in East London, accompanies us.

From Campbell Street there is no evidence left of Deane's Commercial Hotel. The whole building has been converted into shops. The cottage at the back appears to be intact, but obscured by a high wall surrounding it. The backyard is just a fenced-in area. The plot of land across the road where we grew vegetables has a new house on it. The big tree next to where the chicken pen used to be is still standing and looks healthy.

The town hall across the road has received a coat of paint, but the clock is still not working. The Grove Park is totally gone and is now a large parking space surrounded by shops. On the other side, the Emgwenyeni flats looks even more run-down. The town square is still littered with refuse and there is no water in the fountain. The rose garden, although bedraggled, still exists.

The Savoy Hotel is closed, so we are not able to view the UFO memorabilia and stories in the UFO Bar. Bennie Smit now owns the Savoy. While he was away on holidays, supposedly, the locals named the bar UFO Bar. That displeased him greatly, but when the locals threatened a boycott, he agreed to maintain the new name. Next to the Savoy, a doctor's surgery is also closed. In the window of the surgery a notice with a drawing of a large handgun is accompanied by 'No cash kept on premises'.

Across the road is the Fort Beaufort Museum. We enter the museum. I am hoping to get more material for my story. Much of the contents including the old clothing from the nineteenth century, old photographs, paintings, guns and assegais remain as I recall them, but at the back they are in the process of reconstructing the blacksmith's workshop. The son of Mr Aylesbury has donated the contents of the workshop, including the huge bellows, to the museum. A few old organs and pianos have also been donated.

There are many old photographs of rugby teams, crickets teams and past mayors, but my father is missing. The curator says the photos of all the past mayors in the town hall have been taken down by one of the recent mayors.

We drive out of town on the road towards Katberg, past Newtown, to the new golf course to have lunch. It is a well-maintained course with green fairways and putting greens. A few goats are delicately picking leaves from between the sharp thorns of mimosa trees next to the clubhouse.

Inside is a plaque with names of past cricket club presidents and captains. Max Alperstein 1961, 1962, 1963. Two years later, he died.

On the wall of the dining and drinking area is the head of a large kudu and opposite a wooden board with the names of all those who have donated money to the club. Many names are familiar: the Roberts brothers, McComb, Webster, Bezuidenhout and others.

'How much to get our names on the wall?' Neil asks the young barman.

'Only fifty rand.'

'Here's fifty. Just put "The Alperstein Family".'

We continue our pilgrimage to the barrage, the two swing bridges crossing the Kat and Brak rivers and the swimming pool. The swing bridge below the museum is no longer functional and the one near Roger Crane's parents' house is just passable, with many slats of wood missing or broken. Neil and I walk halfway across and decide to turn back – too dangerous. The area around the bridge appears to be used as an open tip for garbage and smells as if it is also used as a toilet.

The day becomes increasingly hot and oppressive. Everything this time round seems to be on a smaller scale compared to what I remember from previous visits and, as expected, much smaller than my childhood memories. The town square looks smaller, the area where the park had been looks smaller, the space the hotel had occupied looks smaller.

'Even the mental hospital looks smaller,' I remark.

'That's not where the mental hospital was. The mental hospital is those buildings across the Kat River the other side of the old swing bridge,' insists Melanie. 'The Queen used to take me there to get my hair cut.'

'That's the new section. Where Ellie took me to watch the Xhosa patients get shock treatment is that building,' I reply.

'Neil, which is the building where we used to tease George Paraffin?' asks Melanie.

'That one.' He points to the old building I have been looking at.

'On the left side, the hotel building went up to there, Andrew,' one of us says.

'No, it ended there,' pointing to another spot says another of us.

Of practically everything we look at and comment on, either my sister, my brother or I have a different recollection.

'So how do you feel about Fort Beaufort now that you've done your nostalgia trip around town?' enquires Andrew.

Neil has been looking progressively more uncomfortable. 'I didn't want to come back and see Fort Beaufort as different and deteriorated as it is. I wanted to keep my childhood memories of this place. The only reason I came was so that Eli and the kids could see where I grew up. I find this all too depressing.'

'I don't think Fort Beaufort has changed at all,' says Melanie.

The hotel in which we grew up is no longer there; the park where we spent many hours on our bicycles destroying the elephant grass hedges is no longer there; the swing bridges are no longer passable. The streets now look more like a 'rainbow nation' than a 'white' colonial country town.

44

The end finishes
At the beginning
In a flash

'Excuse me, would you please take a photograph of us in front of this building?' requests Neil of a young Xhosa woman.

Hesitantly, she takes my brother's camera from his hand, looking perplexed. Through the lens she focuses her gaze on the three people, two men and a woman, standing in front of the relic of the hotel. In an awkward silence, the wind rustles plastic bags littering the street. A few yards away, a stray dog nonchalantly chews on chicken bones in the gutter.

The woman steadies the camera and presses the button.

'We used to live here,' says my brother.

She hands back the camera with a puzzled smile. She walks down the street shaking her head.

Postscript

Neil did not become an astronaut, nor was he involved in space travel, but became an architect. He married Eli Jakobson, a Norwegian whom he met in Cape Town. She had spent many years in a number of African countries working for a Norwegian NGO doing AIDS education in schools. Currently they live in Norway with their two children Amelie and Sofia.

Melanie became a nurse with multiple qualifications and degrees, and currently is a lecturer in primary health care at the medical school at the University of Cape Town. Her son Batandwa is the same age as our elder son Dion. Both Melanie and Neil had left South Africa for a few years in the 1970s but returned in the early 80s.

I spent most of my working life as a paediatrician with a subspecialty in child public health for half of it. Melissa, who is an artist, and I left South Africa in January 1977 and lived in the USA for thirteen years, eleven of those in New York City. While in New York, Melissa did many paintings that related to the struggle in South Africa. Four paintings now belong to the Ifa Lethu Foundation and have been represented in international exhibitions of Art Against Apartheid. In 1990, three years after our elder son Dion was born, we moved to Sydney, Australia, where our second son Lucien was born and where we have lived since.

Select Bibliography

In preparation for the historical fiction components of the story, I read in part or whole the following books and articles.

Bennun, N., *The Broken String: The Last Words of an Extinct People*. Penguin Books, 2005.

Boonzaier, E., Berens P., Malherbe C. & Smith A., *The Cape Herders: A history of the Khoikhoi of Southern Africa*. David Philip Publ., Cape Town, 1996.

Cape melting pot. The role and status of the mixed population at the cape 1652–1795 as translated by Delia A. Robertson from *Groep Sonder Grense* by H.F. Heese MA PhD.

Elbourne, E. *Blood Ground. Colonialism, Missions, and the Contest for Christianity in the Cape Colony and Britain, 1799–1853*. McGill-Queen's University Press, 2002.

Elliot, A. *The Magic World of the Xhosa*. Collins, Cape Town, 1970.

Fort Beaufort, *Golden Walkway. Amatola Heritage Initiative*. Amatola District Council, Fort Beaufort Historical Museum.

Guelke, L. & Shell, R., *Landscape of Conquest: Frontier Water Alienation and Khoikhoi Strategies of Survival, 1652–1780 Journal of Southern African Studies*, Vol. 18, No. 4, December 1992.

Hopkins, H.C., *A Concise History of the Foundation and Development of Fort Beaufort*. Fort Beaufort *Advocate*, February 1952.

Marshall, Thomas E., *The Harmless People*. Africasouth Paperbacks, David Philip Publ., Cape Town, 1988.

Matthews, H.T., *A Guide and History of Fort Beaufort*. Dutch Reformed Church of the Transvaal, 1958.

Morrell, R., *Changing men in South Africa London*. University of Natal Press, 2001.

Mostert, N., *The Epic of South Africa's Creation and the Tragedy of the Xhosa People*. Alfred A. Knopf, New York, 1992.

Nel, E.L., & Hill, T.R., eds, *An evaluation of community driven economic development, land tenure and sustainable environmental development in the Kat River Valley*. HSRC Publishers, Pretoria, 2000.

Newton-King, S., & Malherbe, V.C., *The Khoikhoi Rebellion in the Eastern Cape (1799–1803)* Centre for African Studies, University of Cape Town, 1981.

Omer-Cooper, J.D., *History of Southern Africa*, 2nd ed. David Philip Publ., Cape Town, 1994.

Parkington, J., Cederberg *Rock Paintings: Follow the San*. Creda Communications, Cape Town, 2008.

Peires J.B., *The Dead will arise. Nongqawuse and the Great Xhosa Cattle-Killing Movement of 1856–7*. Raven Press, Johannesburg, 1989.

—, *The House of Phalo. A History of the Xhosa People in the Days of their Independence*. Ravan Press, Johannesburg,1987.

—, *The Khoikhoi of the Amathole*. 2009.

—, 'The Legend of Fenner-Solomon'. In *Class, Community and Conflict*. Ed. B. Bozzoli. Ravan Press, Johannesburg, 1987.

Samuel, R., & Thompson, P., T*he myths we live by London*: Routledge, 1990.

Schapera, I., *The Khoisan Peoples of South Africa: Bushmen and Hottentots*. Routledge Publishers, London, 1930.

Sinha, M., Colonial *masculinity, 'The 'manly Englishman' and the 'effeminate Bengali' in the late nineteenth century*. Manchester University Press, 1995.

Sleight, D., *Islands*. Harcourt Books, Orlando USA, 2002.

Soga, J.H., *South-Eastern Bantu. Bantu Studies Suppl 2*. Witwatersrand University Press, 1930.

Stapleton, T.J., 'The Memory of Maqoma: An assessment of Jingqi oral tradition in Ciskei and Transkei'. *History in Africa*, 20:321–325, 1993.

Stow, G.W., *The Native Races of South Africa: a history of the intrusion of the Hottentots and Bantu into the hunting grounds of the Bushmen, the aborigines of the country*. Swan Sonnenschein, London, 1905.

The Great Dance. A Hunters Story (DVD). Aardvark Pictures/Earthrise/Liquid Pictures/Off The Fence Production.

The Journal and Selected Writings of Reverend Tiyo Soga. Ed. Williams, D. Published for Rhodes University. A.A. Balkema, Cape Town, 1983.

The Maqoma Heritage Route. Amatola Heritage Initiative. Amatola District Council. Creative Impact.

The Narrative of Private Buck Adams 7th (Princess Royal's) Dragoon Guards on the Eastern Frontier of the Cape of Good Hope 1843–1848. Ed. A. Gordon Brown. The Van Riebeeck Society, Cape Town, 1941.

Tyrrell, B., *Suspicion is my Name*. Gothic Printing, Cape Town, 1971.

Uhambo Luyazilawula. A Documentary (DVD). The Amatola Heritage Initiative. The Amatola District Municipality East London South Africa.

Victor, S., Land Dispossession and Historical Myth: Andries Botha of the Kat River and his Descendents. Unpublished document, 2010.

'War of Ngcayechibi'. Gungubele, Sitokhwe Tyhali and Tini Maqomo: *Case Studies in Resistance*.

Ward, Harriet, *The Cape and The 'Kaffir's: A Diary of Five Years Residence in 'kaffir' land*. 3rd Edition. Henry G. Bohn, York Street, Covent Garden London, 1851.

Weinberg, P., *In Search of the San*. The Porcupine Press, Johannesburg 1997.

West, M., Morris J. Abantu, *An Introduction to the Black People of South Africa*. C. Struik Publ., Cape Town, 1984.

Wilson, Monica, & Thompson, Leonard, eds, *A History of South Africa to 1870*. Croom Helm, London, 1983.

Acknowledgements

I would like to acknowledge and thank the many friends and family (Melanie and Neil Alperstein) for their encouragement and feedback on my story at various points of development, even when I didn't follow their advice.

I would like to thank Smoky Robinson and Ian David for feedback on early versions, and members of the Bondi Writers Group, from whom I regularly received feedback while they still met as a group.

The Randwick Writers Group, a group of five writers, including me, met fortnightly for the past year reviewing each other's work. The encouragement and in-depth editing and comment from Dina Davis, Susan Beinart, Anne Skyvington and Geraldine Star have been invaluable in progressing my skills as a writer and my story.

At one of my mid-novel crises, I received invaluable advice on structure, including an edit of the manuscript from Joline Young from Cape Town, South Africa.

I would like to acknowledge the Government Archives, Parliament of the Republic of South Africa, the Cape Provincial Museum Service, the Fort Beaufort Museum, Round Table 62 (Fort Beaufort), Fort Beaufort van Ouds and Pierre Lotz of Fort Beaufort for providing images and access to images of Fort Beaufort, and Cecile Yazbek for helping organise the images.

I would like to thank my wife, Melissa, for her unconditional support and multiple reviews on the story. She also managed to stop me hitting the delete key on many occasions. Also my children Dion and Lucien, for whom the initial stories were part of their bedtime rituals, for their feedback and encouragement.

I am grateful to Nondumisa Mginywa from Grahamstown, South Africa, for reviewing and correcting my Xhosa translations.

I am also grateful to Maria Kooper and Margrita Otto, native Nama speakers from Keetmanshoop, Namibia, for translating some of the San and Khoi dialogue into Nama, a Khoisan language similar to /Xam. /Xam is now apparently an extinct language that would have been spoken by the San in the Fort Beaufort region.

Finally, I would like to thank all the inhabitants of Fort Beaufort, past and present, real and fictitious, for making the story possible.

www.ingramcontent.com/pod-product-compliance
Lightning Source LLC
Chambersburg PA
CBHW071827080526
44589CB00012B/935